AF345556

"ABE" LINCOLN'S ANECDOTES AND STORIES

LECTOR HOUSE PUBLIC DOMAIN WORKS

This book is a result of an effort made by Lector House towards making a contribution to the preservation and repair of original classic literature. The original text is in the public domain in the United States of America, and possibly other countries depending upon their specific copyright laws.

In an attempt to preserve, improve and recreate the original content, certain conventional norms with regard to typographical mistakes, hyphenations, punctuations and/or other related subject matters, have been corrected upon our consideration. However, few such imperfections might not have been rectified as they were inherited and preserved from the original content to maintain the authenticity and construct, relevant to the work. We believe that this work holds historical, cultural and/or intellectual importance in the literary works community, therefore despite the oddities, we accounted the work for print as a part of our continuing effort towards preservation of literary work and our contribution towards the development of the society as a whole, driven by our beliefs.

We are grateful to our readers for putting their faith in us and accepting our imperfections with regard to preservation of the historical content. We shall strive hard to meet up to the expectations to improve further to provide an enriching reading experience.

Though, we conduct extensive research in ascertaining the status of copyright before redeveloping a version of the content, in rare cases, a classic work might be incorrectly marked as not-in-copyright. In such cases, if you are the copyright holder, then kindly contact us or write to us, and we shall get back to you with an immediate course of action.

HAPPY READING!

"ABE" LINCOLN'S ANECDOTES AND STORIES

ABRAHAM LINCOLN,
R. D. WORDSWORTH

ISBN: 978-93-88396-67-7

First Published: -

© LECTOR HOUSE LLP

LECTOR HOUSE LLP
E-MAIL: lectorpublishing@gmail.com

"ABE" LINCOLN'S ANECDOTES AND STORIES

A COLLECTION OF THE BEST STORIES TOLD BY LINCOLN WHICH MADE HIM FAMOUS AS AMERICA'S BEST STORY TELLER

COMPILED BY

R. D. WORDSWORTH

COMPILED, 1908,
FOR
THE MUTUAL BOOK COMPANY

CONTENTS

ix

CONTENTS

CONTENTS xi

"ABE" LINCOLN'S
ANECDOTES AND STORIES

A FUN-LOVING AND HUMOR-LOVING MAN

It was once said of Shakespeare that the great mind that conceived the tragedies of "Hamlet," "Macbeth," etc., would have lost its reason if it had not found vent in the sparkling humor of such comedies as "The Merry Wives of Windsor" and "The Comedy of Errors."

The great strain on the mind of Abraham Lincoln produced by four years of civil war might likewise have overcome his reason had it not found vent in the yarns and stories he constantly told. No more fun-loving or humor- loving man than Abraham Lincoln ever lived. He enjoyed a joke even when it was on himself, and probably, while he got his greatest enjoyment from telling stories, he had a keen appreciation of the humor in those that were told him.

MATRIMONIAL ADVICE

For a while during the Civil War, General Fremont was without a command. One day in discussing Fremont's case with George W. Julian, President Lincoln said he did not know where to place him, and that it reminded him of the old man who advised his son to take a wife, to which the young man responded: "All right; whose wife shall I take?"

A SLOW HORSE

On one occasion when Mr. Lincoln was going to attend a political convention one of his rivals, a liveryman, provided him with a slow horse, hoping that he would not reach his destination in time. Mr. Lincoln got there, however, and when he returned with the horse he said: "You keep this horse for funerals, don't you?" "Oh, no," replied the liveryman. "Well, I'm glad of that, for if you did you'd never get a corpse to the grave in time for the resurrection."

A VAIN GENERAL

In an interview between President Lincoln and Petroleum V. Nasby, the name came up of a recently deceased politician of Illinois whose merit was blemished by great vanity. His funeral was very largely attended.

"If General — — had known how big a funeral he would have had," said Mr. Lincoln, "he would have died years ago."

HAD CONFIDENCE IN HIM—"BUT"—

"General Blank asks for more men," said Secretary of War Stanton to the President one day, showing the latter a telegram from the commander named, appealing for re-enforcements.

"I guess he's killed off enough men, hasn't he?" queried the President. "I don't mean Confederates—our own men. What's the use in sending volunteers down to him if they're only used to fill graves?"

"His dispatch seems to imply that, in his opinion, you have not the confidence in him he thinks he deserves," the War Secretary went on to say, as he looked over the telegram again.

"Oh," was the President's reply, "he needn't lose any of his sleep on that account. Just telegraph him to that effect; also, that I don't propose to send him any more men."

HARDTACK BETTER THAN GENERALS

Secretary of War Stanton told the President the following story, which greatly amused the latter, as he was especially fond of a joke at the expense of some high military or civil dignitary.

Stanton had little or no sense of humor.

When Secretary Stanton was making a trip up the Broad River in North Carolina, in a tugboat, a Federal picket yelled out, "What have you got on board of that tug?"

The severe and dignified answer was, "The Secretary of War and Major-General Foster."

Instantly the picket roared back, "We've got major-generals enough up here. Why don't you bring us up some hardtack?"

DOUGLAS HELD LINCOLN'S HAT

When Mr. Lincoln delivered his first inaugural he was introduced by his friend, United States Senator E. D. Baker, of Oregon. He carried a cane and a little roll—the manuscript of his inaugural address. There was a moment's pause after the introduction, as he vainly looked for a spot where he might place his high silk hat.

Stephen A. Douglas, the political antagonist of his whole public life, the man who had pressed him hardest in the campaign of 1860, was seated just behind him. Douglas stepped forward quickly, and took the hat which Mr.

Lincoln held helplessly in his hand.

"If I can't be President," Douglas whispered smilingly to Mrs. Brown, a cousin of Mrs. Lincoln and a member of the President's party, "I at least can hold his hat."

HIS PASSES TO RICHMOND NOT HONORED

A man called upon the President and solicited a pass for Richmond.

"Well," said the President, "I would be very happy to oblige, if my passes were respected; but the fact is, sir, I have, within the past two years, given passes to two hundred and fifty thousand men to go to Richmond, and not one has got there yet."

The applicant quietly and respectfully withdrew on his tiptoes.

LINCOLN AS A DANCER

Lincoln made his first appearance in society when he was first sent to Springfield, Ill., as a member of the State Legislature. It was not an imposing figure which he cut in a ballroom, but still he was occasionally to be found there. Miss Mary Todd, who afterward became his wife, was the magnet which drew the tall, awkward young man from his den. One evening Lincoln approached Miss Todd, and said, in his peculiar idiom:

"Miss Todd, I should like to dance with you the worst way."

The young woman accepted the inevitable, and hobbled around the room with him. When she returned to her seat, one of her companions asked mischievously:

"Well, Mary, did he dance with you the worst way?"

"Yes," she answered, "the very worst."

LOVED SOLDIERS' HUMOR

Lincoln loved anything that savored of wit or humor among the soldiers. He used to relate two stories to show, he said, that neither death nor danger could quench the grim humor of the American soldier:

"A soldier of the Army of the Potomac was being carried to the rear of battle with both legs shot off, who, seeing a pie-woman, called out, 'Say, old lady, are them pies sewed or pegged?'

"And there was another one of the soldiers at the battle of Chancellorsville, whose regiment, waiting to be called into the fight, was taking coffee. The hero of the story put to his lips a crockery mug which he had carried with care through several campaigns. A stray bullet, just missing the drinker's head, dashed the mug into fragments and left only the handle on his finger. Turning his head in that direction, he scowled, 'Johnny, you can't do that again!'"

WANTED TO "BORROW" THE ARMY

During one of the periods when things were at a standstill, the Washington authorities, being unable to force General McClellan to assume an aggressive attitude, President Lincoln went to the general's headquarters to have a talk with him, but for some reason he was unable to get an audience.

Mr. Lincoln returned to the White House much disturbed at his failure to see the commander of the Union forces, and immediately sent for two general officers, to have a consultation. On their arrival, he told them he must have some one to talk to about the situation, and as he had failed to see General McClellan, he wished their views as to the possibility or probability of commencing active operations with the Army of the Potomac.

"Something's got to be done," said the President, emphatically, "and done right away, or the bottom will fall out of the whole thing. Now, if McClellan doesn't want to use the army for a while, I'd like to borrow it from him and see if I can't do something or other with it.

"If McClellan can't fish, he ought at least to be cutting bait at a time like this."

"FIXED UP" A BIT FOR THE "CITY FOLKS"

Mrs. Lincoln knew her husband was not "pretty," but she liked to have him presentable when he appeared before the public. Stephen Fiske, in "When Lincoln Was First Inaugurated," tells of Mrs. Lincoln's anxiety to have the President-elect "smoothed down" a little when receiving a delegation that was to greet them upon reaching New York City.

"The train stopped," writes Mr. Fiske, "and through the windows immense crowds could be seen; the cheering drowning the blowing off of steam of the locomotive. Then Mrs. Lincoln opened her handbag and said:

"'Abraham, I must fix you up a bit for these city folks.'

"Mr. Lincoln gently lifted her upon the seat before him; she parted, combed and brushed his hair and arranged his black necktie.

"'Do I look nice now, mother?' he affectionately asked.

"'Well, you'll do, Abraham,' replied Mrs. Lincoln critically. So he kissed her and lifted her down from the seat, and turned to meet Mayor Wood, courtly and suave, and to have his hand shaken by the other New York officials."

"FIND OUT FOR YOURSELVES"

"Several of us lawyers," remarked one of his colleagues, "in the eastern end of the circuit, annoyed Lincoln once while he was holding court for Davis by attempting to defend against a note to which there were many makers. We had no legal, but a good moral defense, but what we wanted most of all was to stave it off till the next term of court by one expedient or another.

"We bothered 'the court' about it till late on Saturday, the day of adjournment. He adjourned for supper with nothing left but this case to dispose of. After supper he heard our twaddle for nearly an hour, and then made this odd entry:

"'L. D. Chaddon vs. J. D. Beasley et al., April Term, 1856. Champaign County Court. Plea in abatement by B. Z. Green, a defendant not served, filed Saturday at 11 o'clock a.m., April 24, 1856, stricken from the files by order of court. Demurrer to declaration, if there ever was one, overruled. Defendants who are served now, at 8 o'clock p.m., of the last day of the term, ask to plead to the merits, which is denied by the court on the ground that the offer comes too late, and therefore, as by nil dicet, judgment is rendered for Pl'ff. Clerk assess damages. A. Lincoln, Judge pro tem.'

"The lawyer who reads this singular entry will appreciate its oddity if no one else does. After making it, one of the lawyers, on recovering from his astonishment, ventured to inquire: 'Well, Lincoln, how can we get this case up again?'

"Lincoln eyed him quizzically for a moment, and then answered, 'You have all been so mighty smart about this case, you can find out how to take it up again yourselves.'"

COLD MOLASSES WAS SWIFTER

"Old Pap," as the soldiers called General George H. Thomas, was aggravatingly slow at a time when the President wanted him to "get a move on"; in fact, the gallant "Rock of Chickamauga" was evidently entered in a snail-race.

"Some of my generals are so slow," regretfully remarked Lincoln one day, "that molasses in the coldest days of winter is a race horse compared to them.

"They're brave enough, but somehow or other they get fastened in a fence corner, and can't figure their way out."

"DON'T KILL HIM WITH YOUR FIST"

Ward Lamon, Marshal of the District of Columbia during Lincoln's time in Washington, was a powerful man; his strength was phenomenal, and a blow from his fist was like unto that coming from the business end of a sledge.

Lamon tells this story, the hero of which is not mentioned by name, but in all probability his identity can be guessed:

"On one occasion, when the fears of the loyal element of the city (Washington) were excited to fever-heat, a free fight near the old National Theatre occurred about eleven o'clock one night. An officer, in passing the place, observed what was going on, and seeing the great number of persons engaged, he felt it to be his duty to command the peace.

"The imperative tone of his voice stopped the fighting for a moment, but the leader, a great bully, roughly pushed back the officer and told him to go away or he would whip him. The officer again advanced and said, 'I arrest you,' attempting to place his hand on the man's shoulder, when the bully struck a fearful blow at the officer's face.

"This was parried, and instantly followed by a blow from the fist of the officer, striking the fellow under the chin and knocking him senseless. Blood issued from his mouth, nose and ears. It was believed that the man's neck was broken. A surgeon was called, who pronounced the case a critical one, and the wounded man was hurried away on a litter to the hospital.

"There the physicians said there was concussion of the brain, and that the man would die. All the medical skill the officer could procure was employed in the hope of saving the life of the man. His conscience smote him for having, as he believed, taken the life of a fellow-creature, and he was inconsolable.

"Being on terms of intimacy with the President, about two o'clock that night the officer went to the White House, woke up Mr. Lincoln, and requested him to come into his office, where he told him his story. Mr. Lincoln listened with great interest until the narrative was completed, and then asked a few questions, after which he remarked:

"'I am sorry you had to kill the man, but these are times of war, and a great many men deserve killing. This one, according to your story, is one of them; so give yourself no uneasiness about the matter. I will stand by you.'

"'That is not why I came to you. I knew I did my duty, and had no fears of your disapproval of what I did,' replied the officer; and then he added: 'Why I came to you was, I felt great grief over the unfortunate affair, and I wanted to talk to you about it.'

"Mr. Lincoln then said, with a smile, placing his hand on the officer's shoulder: 'You go home now and get some sleep; but let me give you this piece of advice—hereafter, when you have occasion to strike a man, don't

hit him with your fist; strike him with a club, a crowbar, or with something that won't kill him.'"

"AND—HERE I AM!"

An old acquaintance of the President visited him in Washington. Lincoln desired to give him a place. Thus encouraged, the visitor, who was an honest man, but wholly inexperienced in public affairs or business, asked for a high office, Superintendent of the Mint.

The President was aghast, and said: "Good gracious! Why didn't he ask to be the Secretary of the Treasury, and have done with it?"

Afterward, he said: "Well, now, I never thought Mr. —— had anything more than average ability, when we were young men together. But, then, I suppose he thought the same thing about me, and—here I am!"

PRAISES HIS RIVAL FOR OFFICE

When Mr. Lincoln was a candidate for the Legislature, it was the practice at that date in Illinois for two rival candidates to travel over the district together. The custom led to much good-natured raillery between them; and in such contests Lincoln was rarely, if ever, worsted. He could even turn the generosity of a rival to account by his whimsical treatment.

On one occasion, says Mr. Weir, a former resident of Sangamon county, he had driven out from Springfield in company with a political opponent to engage in joint debate. The carriage, it seems, belonged to his opponent. In addressing the gathering of farmers that met them, Lincoln was lavish in praise of the generosity of his friend.

"I am too poor to own a carriage," he said, "but my friend has generously invited me to ride with him. I want you to vote for me if you will; but if not, then vote for my opponent, for he is a fine man."

His extravagant and persistent praise of his opponent appealed to the sense of humor in his rural audience, to whom his inability to own a carriage was by no means a disqualification.

HAD TO WAIT FOR HIM

President Lincoln, having arranged to go to New York, was late for his train, much to the disgust of those who were to accompany him, and all were compelled to wait several hours until the next train steamed out of the station. President Lincoln was much amused at the dissatisfaction displayed, and then ventured the remark that the situation reminded him of "a little story." Said he:

"Out in Illinois, a convict who had murdered his cellmate was sentenced to be hanged. On the day set for the execution, crowds lined the roads leading to the spot where the scaffold had been erected, and there was much jostling and excitement. The condemned man took matters coolly, and as one batch of perspiring, anxious men rushed past the cart in which he was riding, he called out, 'Don't be in a hurry, boys. You've got plenty of time. There won't be any fun until I get there.'

"That's the condition of things now," concluded the President; "there won't be any fun at New York until I get there."

MAKE SOMETHING OUT OF IT, ANYWAY

From the day of his nomination by the Chicago convention, gifts poured in upon Lincoln. Many of these came in the form of wearing apparel. Mr. George Lincoln, of Brooklyn, who brought to Springfield, in January, 1861, a handsome silk hat to the President-elect, the gift of a New York hatter, told some friends that in receiving the hat Lincoln laughed heartily over the gifts of clothing, and remarked to Mrs. Lincoln: "Well, wife, if nothing else comes out of this scrape, we are going to have some new clothes, are we not?"

SORRY FOR THE HORSES

When President Lincoln heard of the Confederate raid at Fairfax, in which a brigadier-general and a number of valuable horses were captured, he gravely observed:

"Well, I am sorry for the horses."

"Sorry for the horses, Mr. President!" exclaimed the Secretary of War, raising his spectacles and throwing himself back in his chair in astonishment.

"Yes," replied Mr. Lincoln, "I can make a brigadier-general in five minutes, but it is not easy to replace a hundred and ten horses."

NOISE LIKE A TURNIP

"Every man has his own peculiar and particular way of getting at and do-ing things," said President Lincoln one day, "and he is often criticised because that way is not the one adopted by others. The great idea is to accomplish what you set out to do. When a man is successful in whatever he attempts, he has many imitators, and the methods used are not so closely scrutinized, although no man who is of good intent will resort to mean, underhanded, scurvy tricks.

"That reminds me of a fellow out in Illinois, who had better luck in getting prairie chickens than any one in the neighborhood. He had a rusty old gun no other man dared to handle; he never seemed to exert himself, being listless and indifferent when out after game, but he always brought home all the chick-ens he could carry, while some of the others, with their finely trained dogs and latest improved fowling-pieces, came home alone.

"'How is it, Jake?' inquired one sportsman, who, although a good shot, and knew something about hunting, was often unfortunate, 'that you never come home without a lot of birds?'

"Jake grinned, half closed his eyes, and replied: 'Oh, I don't know that there's anything queer about it. I jes' go ahead an' git 'em.'

"'Yes, I know you do; but how do you do it?'

"'You'll tell.'

"'Honest, Jake, I won't say a word. Hope to drop dead this minute.'

"'Never say nothing, if I tell you?'

"'Cross my heart three times.'

"This reassured Jake, who put his mouth close to the ear of his eager questioner, and said, in a whisper:

"'All you got to do is jes' to hide in a fence corner an' make a noise like a turnip. That'll bring the chickens every time.'"

LET SIX SKUNKS GO

The President had decided to select a new War Minister, and the leading Republican Senators thought the occasion was opportune to change the whole seven Cabinet ministers. They, therefore, earnestly advised him to make a clean sweep, and select seven new men, and so restore the waning confidence of the country.

The President listened with patient courtesy, and when the Senators had concluded, he said, with a characteristic gleam of humor in his eye:

"Gentlemen, your request for a change of the whole Cabinet because I have made one change reminds me of a story I once heard in Illinois, of a farmer who was much troubled by skunks. His wife insisted on his trying to get rid of them.

"He loaded his shotgun one moonlight night and awaited developments. After some time the wife heard the shotgun go off, and in a few minutes the farmer entered the house.

"'What luck have you?' asked she.

"'I hid myself behind the wood-pile,' said the old man, 'with the shotgun pointed towards the hen roost, and before long there appeared not one skunk, but seven. I took aim, blazed away, killed one, and he raised such a fearful smell that I concluded it was best to let the other six go.'"

The Senators laughed and retired.

ONE THING "ABE" DIDN'T LOVE

Lincoln admitted that he was not particularly energetic when it came to real hard work.

"My father," said he one day, "taught me how to work, but not to love it. I never did like to work, and I don't deny it. I'd rather read, tell stories, crack jokes, talk, laugh—anything but work."

THE MAN HE WAS LOOKING FOR

Judge Kelly, of Pennsylvania, who was one of the committee to advise Lincoln of his nomination, and who was himself a great many feet high, had been eyeing Lincoln's lofty form with a mixture of admiration and possibly jealousy.

This had not escaped Lincoln, and as he shook hands with the judge he inquired, "What is your height?"

"Six feet three. What is yours, Mr. Lincoln?" "Six feet four."

"Then," said the judge, "Pennsylvania bows to Illinois. My dear man, for years my heart has been aching for a President that I could look up to, and I've at last found him."

WANTED STANTON SPANKED

Old Dennis Hanks was sent to Washington at one time by persons interested in securing the release from jail of several men accused of being copperheads. It was thought Old Dennis might have some influence with the President.

The latter heard Dennis' story and then said: "I will send for Mr. Stanton. It is his business."

Secretary Stanton came into the room, stormed up and down, and said the men ought to be punished more than they were. Mr. Lincoln sat quietly in his chair and waited for the tempest to subside, and then quietly said to Stanton he would like to have the papers next day.

When he had gone, Dennis said:

"'Abe,' if I was as big and as ugly as you are, I would take him over my knee and spank him."

The President replied: "No, Stanton is an able and valuable man for this Nation, and I am glad to bear his anger for the service he can give the Nation."

SIX FEET FOUR AT SEVENTEEN

"Abe's" school teacher, Crawford, endeavored to teach his pupils some of the manners of the "polite society" of Indiana—1823 or so. This was a part of his system:

One of the pupils would retire, and then come in as a stranger, and another pupil would have to introduce him to all the members of the school in what was considered "good manners."

As "Abe" wore a linsey-woolsey shirt, buckskin breeches which were too short and very tight, and low shoes, and was tall and awkward, he no doubt created considerable merriment when his turn came. He was growing at a fearful rate; he was fifteen years of age, and two years later attained his full height of six feet four inches.

JUST LIKE SEWARD

The first corps of the army commanded by General Reynolds was once reviewed by the President on a beautiful plain at the north of Potomac Creek, about eight miles from Hooker's headquarters. The party rode thither in an ambulance over a rough corduroy road, and as they passed over some of the more difficult portions of the jolting way the ambulance driver, who sat well in front, occasionally let fly a volley of suppressed oaths at his wild team of six mules.

Finally, Mr. Lincoln, leaning forward, touched the man on the shoulder and said:

"Excuse me, my friend, are you an Episcopalian?" The

man, greatly startled, looked around and replied: "No, Mr.

President; I am a Methodist."

"Well," said Lincoln, "I thought you must be an Episcopalian, because you swear just like Governor Seward, who is a church warden."

"ABE" GOT THE WORST OF IT

When Lincoln was a young lawyer in Illinois, he and a certain judge once got to bantering one another about trading horses; and it was agreed that the next morning at nine o'clock they should make a trade, the horses to be unseen up to that hour, and no backing out, under a forfeiture of $25. At the hour appointed, the Judge came up, leading the sorriest-looking specimen of a horse ever seen in those parts. In a few minutes Mr. Lincoln was seen approaching with a wooden saw-horse upon his shoulders.

Great were the shouts and laughter of the crowd, and both were greatly increased when Lincoln, on surveying the Judge's animal, set down his saw-horse and exclaimed:

"Well, Judge, this is the first time I ever got the worst of it in a horse trade."

HE "SET 'EM UP"

Immediately after Mr. Lincoln's nomination for President at the Chicago convention, a Committee, of which Governor Morgan, of New York, was chairman, visited him in Springfield, Ill., where he was officially informed of his nomination.

After this ceremony had passed, Mr. Lincoln remarked to the company that as a fit ending to an interview so important and interesting as that which had just taken place, he supposed good manners would require that he should treat the committee with something to drink; and opening the door that led into the rear, he called out, "Mary! Mary!" A girl responded to the call, to whom Mr. Lincoln spoke a few words in an undertone, and, closing the door, returned again and talked with his guests. In a few minutes the maid entered, bearing a large waiter, containing several glass tumblers, and a large pitcher, and placed them upon the center-table. Mr. Lincoln arose, and gravely addressing the company, said: "Gentlemen, we must pledge our mutual health in the most healthy beverage that God has given to man—it is the only beverage I have ever used or allowed my family to use, and I cannot conscientiously depart from it on the present occasion. It is pure Adam's ale from the spring." And, taking the tumbler, he touched it to his lips, and pledged them his highest respects in a cup of cold water. Of course, all his guests admired his consistency, and joined in his example.

GOD WITH A LITTLE "G"

> Abraham Lincoln his hand
> and pen
>> he will be good
>>> but god Knows When

These lines were found written in young Lincoln's own hand at the bottom of a page whereon he had been ciphering. Lincoln always wrote a clear, regular "fist." In this instance he evidently did not appreciate the sacredness of the name of the Deity, when he used a little "g."

Lincoln once said he did not remember the time when he could not write.

WHAT AILED THE BOYS

Mr. Roland Diller, who was one of Mr. Lincoln's neighbors in Springfield, tells the following:

"I was called to the door one day by the cries of children in the street, and there was Mr. Lincoln, striding by with two of his boys, both of whom were wailing aloud. 'Why, Mr. Lincoln, what's the matter with the boys?' I asked.

"'Just what's the matter with the whole world,' Lincoln replied. 'I've got three walnuts, and each wants two.'"

"MAJOR-GENERAL, I RECKON"

At one time the President had the appointment of a large additional number of brigadier and major-generals. Among the immense number of applications, Mr. Lincoln came upon one wherein the claims of a certain worthy (not in the service at all) "for a generalship" were glowingly set forth. But the applicant didn't specify whether he wanted to be brigadier or major-general.

The President observed this difficulty, and solved it by a lucid indorsement. The clerk, on receiving the paper again, found written across its back, "Major-General, I reckon. A. Lincoln."

IT TICKLED THE LITTLE WOMAN

Lincoln had been in the telegraph office at Springfield during the casting of the first and second ballots in the Republican National Convention at Chicago, and then left and went over to the office of the State Journal, where he was sitting conversing with friends while the third ballot was being taken.

In a few moments came across the wires the announcement of the result. The superintendent of the telegraph company wrote on a scrap of paper: "Mr. Lincoln, you are nominated on the third ballot," and a boy ran with the message to Lincoln.

He looked at it in silence, amid the shouts of those around him; then rising and putting it in his pocket, he said quietly: "There's a little woman down at our house would like to hear this; I'll go down and tell her."

HE'D SEE IT AGAIN

About two years before Lincoln was nominated for the Presidency he went to Bloomington, Illinois, to try a case of some importance. His opponent— who afterward reached a high place in his profession—was a young man of ability, sensible but sensitive, and one to whom the loss of a case was a great blow. He therefore studied hard and made much preparation.

This particular case was submitted to the jury late at night, and, although anticipating a favorable verdict, the young attorney spent a sleepless night in anxiety. Early next morning he learned, to his great chagrin, that he had lost the case.

Lincoln met him at the court-house some time after the jury had come in, and asked him what had become of his case.

With lugubrious countenance and in a melancholy tone the young man replied, "It's gone to hell."

"Oh, well," replied Lincoln, "then you will see it again."

SURE CURE FOR BOILS

President Lincoln and Postmaster-General Blair were talking of the war. "Blair," said the President, "did you ever know that fright has sometimes proven a cure for boils?" "No, Mr. President, how is that?" "I'll tell you. Not long ago when a colonel, with his cavalry, was at the front, and the Rebs were making things rather lively for us, the colonel was ordered out to a reconnoissance. He was troubled at the time with a big boil where it made horseback riding decidedly uncomfortable. He finally dismounted and ordered the troops forward without him. Soon he was startled by the rapid reports of pistols and the helter-skelter approach of his troops in full retreat before a yelling rebel force. He forgot everything but the yells, sprang into his saddle, and made capital time over the fences and ditches till safe within the lines. The pain from his boil was gone, and the boil too, and the colonel swore that there was no cure for boils so sure as fright from rebel yells."

JUSTICE VS. NUMBERS

Lincoln was constantly bothered by members of delegations of "goody-goodies," who knew all about running the War, but had no inside information as to what was going on. Yet they poured out their advice in streams, until the President was heartily sick of the whole business, and wished the War would find some way to kill off these nuisances.

"How many men have the Confederates now in the field?" asked one of these bores one day.

"About one million two hundred thousand," replied the President.

"Oh, my! Not so many as that, surely, Mr. Lincoln."

"They have fully twelve hundred thousand, no doubt of it. You see, all of our generals when they get whipped say the enemy outnumbers them from three or five to one, and I must believe them. We have four hundred thousand men in the field, and three times four make twelve,—don't you see it? It is as plain to be seen as the nose on a man's face; and at the rate things are now going, with the great amount of speculation and the small crop of fighting, it will take a long time to overcome twelve hundred thousand rebels in arms.

"If they can get subsistence they have everything else, except a just cause. Yet it is said that 'thrice is he armed that hath his quarrel just.' I am willing, however, to risk our advantage of thrice in justice against their thrice in numbers."

LINCOLN SAW STANTON ABOUT IT

Mr. Lovejoy, heading a committee of Western men, discussed an important scheme with the President, and the gentlemen were then directed to explain it to Secretary of War Stanton.

Upon presenting themselves to the Secretary, and showing the President's order, the Secretary said: "Did Lincoln give you an order of that kind?"

"He did, sir."

"Then he is a d—d fool," said the angry Secretary.

"Do you mean to say that the President is a d—d fool?" asked Lovejoy in amazement.

"Yes, sir, if he gave you such an order as that."

The bewildered Illinoisan betook himself at once to the President and related the result of the conference.

"Did Stanton say I was a d—d fool?" asked Lincoln at the close of the recital.

"He did, sir, and repeated it."

After a moment's pause, and looking up, the President said: "If Stanton said I was a d—d fool, then I must be one, for he is nearly always right, and generally says what he means. I will slip over and see him."

SLEEP STANDING UP

McClellan was a thorn in Lincoln's side—"always up in the air," as the President put it—and yet he hesitated to remove him. "The Young Napoleon" was a good organizer, but no fighter. Lincoln sent him everything necessary in the way of men, ammunition, artillery and equipments, but he was forever unready.

Instead of making a forward movement at the time expected, he would notify the President that he must have more men. These were given him as rapidly as possible, and then would come a demand for more horses, more this and that, usually winding up with a demand for still "more men."

Lincoln bore it all in patience for a long time, but one day, when he had received another request for more men, he made a vigorous protest.

"If I gave McClellan all the men he asks for," said the President, "they couldn't find room to lie down. They'd have to sleep standing up."

"ABE'S" LITTLE JOKE

When General W. T. Sherman, November 12th, 1864, severed all communication with the North and started for Savannah with his magnificent army of sixty thousand men, there was much anxiety for a month as to his whereabouts. President Lincoln, in response to an inquiry, said: "I know what hole Sherman went in at, but I don't know what hole he'll come out at."

Colonel McClure had been in consultation with the President one day, about two weeks after Sherman's disappearance, and in this connection related this incident:

"I was leaving the room, and just as I reached the door the President turned around, and, with a merry twinkling of the eye, inquired, 'McClure, wouldn't you like to hear something from Sherman?'

"The inquiry electrified me at the instant, as it seemed to imply that Lincoln had some information on the subject. I immediately answered, 'Yes, most of all, I should like to hear from Sherman.'

"To this President Lincoln answered, with a hearty laugh: 'Well, I'll be hanged if I wouldn't myself.'"

HOW "FIGHTING JOE" WAS APPOINTED

General "Joe" Hooker, the fourth commander of the noble but unfortunate Army of the Potomac, was appointed to that position by President Lincoln in January, 1863. General Scott, for some reason, disliked Hooker and would not appoint him. Hooker, after some months of discouraging waiting, decided to return to California, and called to pay his respects to President Lincoln. He was introduced as Captain Hooker, and to the surprise of the President began the following speech:

"Mr. President, my friend makes a mistake. I am not Captain Hooker, but was once Lieutenant-Colonel Hooker of the regular army. I was lately a farmer in California, but since the Rebellion broke out I have been trying to get into service, but I find I am not wanted.

"I am about to return home; but before going, I was anxious to pay my respects to you, and express my wishes for your personal welfare and success in quelling this Rebellion. And I want to say to you a word more.

"I was at Bull Run the other day, Mr. President, and it is no vanity in me to say, I am a darned sight better general than you had on the field."

This was said, not in the tone of a braggart, but of a man who knew what he was talking about. Hooker did not return to California, but in a few weeks Captain Hooker received from the President a commission as Brigadier-General Hooker.

NO OTHERS LIKE THEM

One day an old lady from the country called on President Lincoln, her tanned face peering up to his through a pair of spectacles. Her errand was to present Mr. Lincoln a pair of stockings of her own make a yard long. Kind tears came to his eyes as she spoke to him, and then, holding the stockings one in each hand, dangling wide apart for general inspection, he assured her that he should take them with him to Washington, where (and here his eyes twinkled) he was sure he should not be able to find any like them.

Quite a number of well-known men were in the room with the President when the old lady made her presentation. Among them was George S. Boutwell, who afterwards became Secretary of the Treasury.

The amusement of the company was not at all diminished by Mr. Boutwell's remark, that the lady had evidently made a very correct estimate of Mr. Lincoln's latitude and longitude.

THE DANDY AND THE BOYS

President Lincoln appointed as consul to a South American country a young man from Ohio who was a dandy. A wag met the new appointee on his way to the White House to thank the President. He was dressed in the most extravagant style. The wag horrified him by telling him that the country to which he was assigned was noted chiefly for the bugs that abounded there and made life unbearable.

"They'll bore a hole clean through you before a week has passed," was the comforting assurance of the wag as they parted at the White House steps. The new consul approached Lincoln with disappointment clearly written all over his face. Instead of joyously thanking the President, he told him the wag's story of the bugs. "I am informed, Mr. President," he said, "that the place is full of vermin and that they could eat me up in a week's time." "Well, young man," replied Lincoln, "if that's true, all I've got to say is that if such a thing happened they would leave a mighty good suit of clothes behind."

BOAT HAD TO STOP

Lincoln never failed to take part in all political campaigns in Illinois, as his reputation as a speaker caused his services to be in great demand. As was natural, he was often the target at which many of the "Smart Alecks" of that period shot their feeble bolts, but Lincoln was so ready with his answers that few of them cared to engage him a second time.

In one campaign Lincoln was frequently annoyed by a young man who entertained the idea that he was a born orator. He had a loud voice, was full of language, and so conceited that he could not understand why the people did not recognize and appreciate his abilities.

This callow politician delighted in interrupting public speakers, and at last Lincoln determined to squelch him. One night while addressing a large meeting at Springfield, the fellow became so offensive that "Abe" dropped the threads of his speech and turned his attention to the tormentor.

"I don't object," said Lincoln, "to being interrupted with sensible questions, but I must say that my boisterous friend does not always make inquiries which properly come under that head. He says he is afflicted with headaches, at which I don't wonder, as it is a well-known fact that nature abhors a vacuum, and takes her own way of demonstrating it.

"This noisy friend reminds me of a certain steamboat that used to run on the Illinois River. It was an energetic boat, was always busy. When they built it, however, they made one serious mistake, this error being in the relative sizes of the boiler and the whistle. The latter was usually busy too, and people were aware that it was in existence.

"This particular boiler to which I have reference was a six-foot one, and did all that was required of it in the way of pushing the boat along; but as the builders of the vessel had made the whistle a six-foot one, the consequence was that every time the whistle blew the boat had to stop."

RAN AWAY WHEN VICTORIOUS

Three or four days after the battle of Bull Run, some gentlemen who had been on the field called upon the President.

He inquired very minutely regarding all the circumstances of the affair, and, after listening with the utmost attention, said, with a touch of humor:

"So it is your notion that we whipped the rebels and then ran away from them!"

HE "SKEWED" THE LINE

When a surveyor, Mr. Lincoln first platted the town of Petersburg, Ill. Some twenty or thirty years afterward the property-owners along one of the outlying streets had trouble in fixing their boundaries. They consulted the official plat and got no relief. A committee was sent to Springfield to consult the distinguished surveyor, but he failed to recall anything that would give them aid, and could only refer them to the record. The dispute therefore went into the courts. While the trial was pending, an old Irishman named McGuire, who had worked for some farmer during the summer, returned to town for the winter. The case being mentioned in his presence, he promptly said: "I can tell you all about it. I helped carry the chain when Abe Lincoln laid out this town. Over there where they are quarreling about the lines, when he was locating the street, he straightened up from his instrument and said: 'If I run that street right through, it will cut three or four feet off the end of — —'s house. It's all he's got in the world and he could never get another. I reckon it won't hurt anything out here if I skew the line a little and miss him.'"

The line was "skewed," and hence the trouble, and more testimony furnished as to Lincoln's abounding kindness of heart, that would not willingly harm any human being.

"HOW DO YOU GET OUT OF THIS PLACE?"

"It seems to me," remarked the President one day while reading over some of the appealing telegrams sent to the War Department by General Mc-Clellan, "that McClellan has been wandering around and has sort of got lost. He's been hollering for help ever since he went South—wants somebody to come to his deliverance and get him out of the place he's got into.

"He reminds me of the story of a man out in Illinois who, in company with a number of friends, visited the State penitentiary. They wandered all through the institution and saw everything, but just about the time to depart this particular man became separated from his friends and couldn't find his way out.

"He roamed up and down one corridor after another, becoming more desperate all the time, when, at last, he came across a convict who was looking out from between the bars of his cell-door. Here was salvation at last. Hurrying up to the prisoner he hastily asked:

"'Say! How do you get out of this place?'"

HELL A MILE FROM THE WHITE HOUSE

Ward Lamon told this story of President Lincoln, whom he found one day in a particularly gloomy frame of mind. Lamon said:

"The President remarked, as I came in, 'I fear I have made Senator Wade, of Ohio, my enemy for life.'

"'How?' I asked.

"'Well,' continued the President, 'Wade was here just now urging me to dismiss Grant, and, in response to something he said, I remarked, "Senator, that reminds me of a story."'

"'What did Wade say,' I inquired of the President.

"'He said, in a petulant way,' the President responded, '"It is with you, sir, all story, story! You are the father of every military blunder that has been made during the war. You are on your road to hell, sir, with this government, by your obstinacy, and you are not a mile off this minute.'"

"'What did you say then?'

"'I good-naturedly said to him,' the President replied, '"Senator, that is just about from here to the Capitol, is it not?" He was very angry, grabbed up his hat and cane, and went away.'"

'TWAS "MOVING DAY"

Speed, who was a prosperous young merchant of Springfield, reports that Lincoln's personal effects consisted of a pair of saddle-bags, containing two or three lawbooks, and a few pieces of clothing. Riding on a borrowed horse, he thus made his appearance in Springfield. When he discovered that a single bedstead would cost seventeen dollars he said, "It is probably cheap enough, but I have not enough money to pay for it." When Speed offered to trust him, he said: "If I fail here as a lawyer, I will probably never pay you at all." Then Speed offered to share a large double bed with him.

"Where is your room?" Lincoln asked.

"Upstairs," said Speed, pointing from the store leading to his room. Without saying a word, he took his saddle-bags on his arm, went upstairs, set them down on the floor, came down again, and with a face beaming with pleasure and smiles, exclaimed: "Well, Speed, I'm moved."

"ABE'S" HAIR NEEDED COMBING

"By the way," remarked President Lincoln one day to Colonel Cannon, a close personal friend, "I can tell you a good story about my hair. When I was nominated at Chicago, an enterprising fellow thought that a great many people would like to see how 'Abe' Lincoln looked, and, as I had not long before sat for a photograph, the fellow, having seen it, rushed over and bought the negative.

"He at once got no end of wood-cuts, and so active was their circulation that they were soon selling in all parts of the country.

"Soon after they reached Springfield, I heard a boy crying them for sale on the streets. 'Here's your likeness of "Abe" Lincoln!' he shouted. 'Buy one; price only two shillings! Will look a great deal better when he gets his hair combed!'"

RIGHT FOR ONCE, ANYHOW

Where men bred in courts, accustomed to the world, or versed in diplomacy, would use some subterfuge, or would make a polite speech, or give a shrug of the shoulders, as the means of getting out of an embarrassing position, Lincoln raised a laugh by some bold west-country anecdote, and moved off in the cloud of merriment produced by the joke. When Attorney-General Bates was remonstrating apparently against the appointment of some indifferent lawyer to a place of judicial importance, the President interposed with: "Come now, Bates, he's not half as bad as you think. Besides that, I must tell you, he did me a good turn long ago. When I took to the law I was going to court one morning, with some ten or twelve miles of bad road before me, and I had no horse.

"The Judge overtook me in his carriage.

"'Hallo, Lincoln! are you not going to the court-house? Come in and I will give you a seat!'

"Well, I got in, and the Judge went on reading his papers. Presently the carriage struck a stump on one side of the road, then it hopped off to the other. I looked out, and I saw the driver was jerking from side to side in his seat, so I says:

"'Judge, I think your coachman has been taking a little too much this morning.'

"'Well, I declare, Lincoln,' said he, 'I should not much wonder if you were right, for he has nearly upset me half a dozen times since starting.'

"So, putting his head out of the window, he shouted, 'Why, you infernal scoundrel, you are drunk!'

"Upon which, pulling up his horses, and turning around with great gravity, the coachman said:

"'Begorra! that's the first rightful decision that you have given for the last twelvemonth.'"

While the company were laughing, the President beat a quiet retreat from the neighborhood.

"SMELT NO ROYALTY IN OUR CARRIAGE"

On one occasion, in going to meet an appointment in the southern part of the Sucker State—that section of Illinois called Egypt—Lincoln, with other friends, was traveling in the "caboose" of a freight train, when the freight was switched off the main track to allow a special train to pass.

Lincoln's more aristocratic rival (Stephen A. Douglas) was being conveyed to the same town in this special. The passing train was decorated with banners and flags, and carried a band of music, which was playing "Hail to the Chief."

As the train whistled past, Lincoln broke out in a fit of laughter, and said: "Boys, the gentleman in that car evidently smelt no royalty in our carriage."

SOMETHING FOR EVERYONE

It was the President's overweening desire to accommodate all persons who came to him soliciting favors, but the opportunity was never offered until an untimely and unthinking disease, which possessed many of the characteristics of one of the most dreaded maladies, confined him to his bed at the White House.

The rumor spread that the President was afflicted with this disease, while the truth was that it was merely a very mild attack of varioloid. The office-seekers didn't know the facts, and for once the Executive Mansion was clear of them.

One day, a man from the West, who didn't read the papers, but wanted the postoffice in his town, called at the White House. The President, being then practically a well man, saw him. The caller was engaged in a voluble

endeavor to put his capabilities in the most favorable light, when the President interrupted him with the remark that he would be compelled to make the interview short, as his doctor was due.

"Why, Mr. President, are you sick?" queried the visitor.

"Oh, nothing much," replied Mr. Lincoln, "but the physician says he fears the worst."

"What worst, may I ask?"

"Smallpox," was the answer; "but you needn't be scared. I'm only in the first stages now."

The visitor grabbed his hat, sprang from his chair, and without a word bolted for the door.

"Don't be in a hurry," said the President placidly; "sit down and talk awhile."

"Thank you, sir; I'll call again," shouted the Westerner, as he disappeared through the opening in the wall.

"Now, that's the way with people," the President said, when relating the story afterward. "When I can't give them what they want, they're dissatisfied, and say harsh things about me; but when I've something to give to everybody they scamper off."

REMINDED HIM OF "A LITTLE STORY"

When Lincoln's attention was called to the fact that, at one time in his boyhood, he had spelled the name of the Deity with a small "g," he replied:

"That reminds me of a little story. It came about that a lot of Confederate mail was captured by the Union forces, and, while it was not exactly the proper thing to do, some of our soldiers opened several letters written by the Southerners at the front to their people at home.

"In one of these missives the writer, in a postscript, jotted down this assertion:

"'We'll lick the Yanks termorrer, if goddlemity (God Almighty) spares our lives.'

"That fellow was in earnest, too, as the letter was written the day before the second battle of Manassas."

BIG ENOUGH HOG FOR HIM

To a curiosity-seeker who desired a permit to pass the lines to visit the field of Bull Run, after the first battle, Lincoln made the following reply: "A man in Cortlandt county raised a porker of such unusual size that strangers went out of their way to see it.

"One of them the other day met the old gentleman and inquired about the animal.

"'Wall, yes,' the old fellow said, 'I've got such a critter, mi'ty big un; but I guess I'll have to charge you about a shillin' for lookin' at him.'

"The stranger looked at the old man for a minute or so, pulled out the desired coin, handed it to him, and started to go off. 'Hold on,' said the other, 'don't you want to see the hog?'

"'No,' said the stranger; 'I have seen as big a hog as I want to see!'

"And you will find that fact the case with yourself, if you should happen to see a few live rebels there as well as dead ones."

HOW "JAKE" GOT AWAY

One of the last, if not the very last story told by President Lincoln, was to one of his Cabinet who came to see him, to ask if it would be proper to permit "Jake" Thompson to slip through Maine in disguise and embark for Portland.

The President, as usual, was disposed to be merciful, and to permit the arch-rebel to pass unmolested, but Secretary Stanton urged that he should be arrested as a traitor.

"By permitting him to escape the penalties of treason," persisted the War Secretary, "you sanction it." "Well," replied Mr. Lincoln, "let me tell you a story. There was an Irish soldier here last summer, who wanted something to drink stronger than water, and stopped at a drug-shop, where he espied a soda-fountain. 'Mr. Doctor,' said he, 'give me, plase, a glass of soda-wather, an' if yez can put in a few drops of whiskey unbeknown to any one, I'll be obleeged.' Now," continued Mr. Lincoln, "if 'Jake' Thompson is permitted to go through Maine unbeknown to any one, what's the harm? So don't have him arrested."

"ABE" RESENTED THE INSULT

A cashiered officer, seeking to be restored through the power of the executive, became insolent, because the President, who believed the man guilty, would not accede to his repeated requests, at last said, "Well, Mr. President,

I see you are fully determined not to do me justice!"

This was too aggravating even for Mr. Lincoln; rising, he suddenly seized the disgraced officer by the coat collar, and marched him forcibly to the door, saying as he ejected him into the passage:

"Sir, I give you fair warning never to show your face in this room again. I can bear censure, but not insult. I never wish to see your face again."

STORIES BETTER THAN DOCTORS

A gentleman, visiting a hospital at Washington, heard an occupant of one of the beds laughing and talking about the President, who had been there a short time before and gladdened the wounded with some of his stories. The soldier seemed in such good spirits that the gentleman inquired:

"You must be very slightly wounded?"

"Yes," replied the brave fellow, "very slightly—I have only lost one leg, and I'd be glad enough to lose the other, if I could hear some more of 'Old Abe's' stories."

"ALL SICKER'N YOUR MAN"

A Commissioner to the Hawaiian Islands was to be appointed, and eight applicants had filed their papers, when a delegation from the South appeared at the White House on behalf of a ninth. Not only was their man fit—so the delegation urged—but was also in bad health, and a residence in that balmy climate would be of great benefit to him.

The President was rather impatient that day, and before the members of the delegation had fairly started in, suddenly closed the interview with this remark:

"Gentlemen, I am sorry to say that there are eight other applicants for that place, and they are all 'sicker'n' your man."

"DID YE ASK MORRISSEY YET?"

John Morrissey, the noted prize fighter, was the "Boss" of Tammany Hall during the Civil War period. It pleased his fancy to go to Congress, and his obedient constituents sent him there. Morrissey was such an absolute despot that the New York City democracy could not make a move without his consent, and many of the Tammanyites were so afraid of him that they would not even enter into business ventures without consulting the autocrat.

President Lincoln had been seriously annoyed by some of his generals, who were afraid to make the slightest move before asking advice from Washington. One commander, in particular, was so cautious that he telegraphed the War Department upon the slightest pretext, the result being that his troops were lying in camp doing nothing, when they should have been in the field.

"This general reminds me," the President said one day, while talking to Secretary Stanton, at the War Department, "of a story I once heard about a Tammany man. He happened to meet a friend, also a member of Tammany, on the street, and in the course of the talk the friend, who was beaming with smiles and good nature, told the other Tammanyite that he was going to be married.

"This first Tammany man looked more serious than men usually do upon hearing of the impending happiness of a friend. In fact, his face seemed to take on a look of anxiety and worry.

"'Ain't you glad to know that I'm to get married?' demanded the second Tammanyite, somewhat in a huff.

"'Of course I am,' was the reply; 'but,' putting his mouth close to the ear of the other, 'have ye asked Morrissey yet?'

"Now this general of whom we are speaking, wouldn't dare order out the guard without asking Morrissey," concluded the President.

LINCOLN ASKED TO BE SHOT

Lincoln was, naturally enough, much surprised one day, when a man of rather forbidding countenance drew a revolver and thrust the weapon into his face. In such circumstances "Abe" at once concluded that any attempt at debate or argument was a waste of time and words.

"What seems to be the matter?" inquired Lincoln with all the calmness and self-possession he could muster.

"Well," replied the stranger, who did not appear at all excited, "some years ago I swore an oath that if I ever came across an uglier man than myself I'd shoot him on the spot."

A feeling of relief evidently took possession of Lincoln at this rejoinder, as the expression upon his countenance lost all suggestion of anxiety.

"Shoot me," he said to the stranger; "for if I am an uglier man than you I don't want to live."

HE COULDN'T WAIT FOR THE COLONEL

General Fisk, attending a reception at the White House, saw waiting in the anteroom a poor old man from Tennessee, and learned that he had been waiting three or four days to get an audience, on which probably depended the life of his son, under sentence of death for some military offense.

General Fisk wrote his case in outline on a card and sent it in, with a special request that the President would see the man. In a moment the order came; and past impatient senators, governors and generals, the old man went.

He showed his papers to Mr. Lincoln, who said he would look into the case and give him the result next day.

The old man, in an agony of apprehension, looked up into the President's sympathetic face and actually cried out:

"Tomorrow may be too late! My son is under sentence of death. It ought to be decided now!"

His streaming tears told how much he was moved.

"Come," said Mr. Lincoln, "wait a bit and I'll tell you a story;" and then he told the old man General Fisk's story about the swearing driver, as follows:

"The general had begun his military life as a colonel, and when he raised his regiment in Missouri he proposed to his men that he should do all the swearing of the regiment. They assented; and for months no instance was known of the violation of the promise.

"The colonel had a teamster named John Todd, who, as roads were not always the best, had some difficulty in commanding his temper and his tongue.

"John happened to be driving a mule team through a series of mudholes a little worse than usual, when, unable to restrain himself any longer, he burst forth into a volley of energetic oaths.

"The colonel took notice of the offense and brought John to account.

"'John,' said he, 'didn't you promise to let me do all the swearing of the regiment?'

"'Yes, I did, colonel,' he replied, 'but the fact was, the swearing had to be done then or not at all, and you weren't there to do it.'"

As he told the story the old man forgot his boy, and both the President and his listener had a hearty laugh together at its conclusion.

Then he wrote a few words which the old man read, and in which he found new occasion for tears; but the tears were tears of joy, for the words saved the life of his son.

HE LOVED A GOOD STORY

Judge Breese, of the Supreme bench, one of the most distinguished of American jurists, and a man of great personal dignity, was about to open court at Springfield, when Lincoln called out in his hearty way: "Hold on, Breese! Don't open court yet! Here's Bob Blackwell just going to tell a story!" The Judge passed on without replying, evidently regarding it as beneath the dignity of the Supreme Court to delay proceedings for the sake of a story.

THE DEAD MAN SPOKE

Mr. Lincoln once said in a speech: "Fellow citizens, my friend, Mr. Douglas, made the startling announcement today that the Whigs are all dead.

"If that be so, fellow-citizens, you will now experience the novelty of hearing a speech from a dead man; and I suppose you might properly say, in the language of the old hymn:

"'Hark! from the tombs a doleful sound.'"

LINCOLN PRONOUNCED THIS STORY FUNNY

The President was heard to declare one day that the story given below was one of the funniest he ever heard.

One of General Fremont's batteries of eight Parrott guns, supported by a squadron of horse commanded by Major Richards, was in sharp conflict with a battery of the enemy near at hand. Shells and shot were flying thick and fast, when the commander of the battery, a German, one of Fremont's staff, rode suddenly up to the cavalry, exclaiming, in loud and excited terms, "Pring up de shackasses! Pring up de shackasses! For Cot's sake, hurry up the shackasses, im-me-di-ate-ly!"

The necessity of this order, though not quite apparent, will be more obvious when it is remembered that "shackasses" are mules, carry mountain howitzers, which are fired from the back of that much-abused but valuable animal; and the immediate occasion for the "shackasses" was that two regiments of rebel infantry were at that moment discovered ascending a hill immediately behind our batteries.

The "shackasses," with the howitzers loaded with grape and canister, were soon on the ground.

The mules squared themselves, as they well knew how, for the shock.

A terrific volley was poured into the advancing column, which immediately broke and retreated.

Two hundred and seventy-eight dead bodies were found in the ravine next day, piled closely together as they fell, the effects of that volley from the backs of the "shackasses."

"PLOUGH ALL 'ROUND HIM"

Governor Blank went to the War Department one day in a towering rage:

"I suppose you found it necessary to make large concessions to him, as he returned from you perfectly satisfied," suggested a friend.

"Oh, no," the President replied, "I did not concede anything. You have heard how that Illinois farmer got rid of a big log that was too big to haul out, too knotty to split, and too wet and soggy to burn.

"'Well, now,' said he, in response to the inquiries of his neighbors one Sunday, as to how he got rid of it, 'well, now, boys, if you won't divulge the secret, I'll tell you how I got rid of it—I ploughed around it.'

"Now," remarked Lincoln, in conclusion, "don't tell anybody, but that's the way I got rid of Governor Blank. I ploughed all round him, but it took me three mortal hours to do it, and I was afraid every minute he'd see what I was at."

"I'VE LOST MY APPLE"

During a public "reception," a farmer from one of the border counties of Virginia told the President that the Union soldiers, in passing his farm, had helped themselves not only to hay, but to his horse, and he hoped the President would urge the proper officer to consider his claim immediately.

Mr. Lincoln said that this reminded him of an old acquaintance of his, "Jack" Chase, a lumberman on the Illinois, a steady, sober man, and the best raftsman on the river. It was quite a trick to take the logs over the rapids; but he was skilful with a raft and always kept her straight in her channel. Finally a steamer was put on, and "Jack" was made captain of her. He always used to take the wheel, going through the rapids. One day when the boat was plunging and wallowing along the boiling current, and "Jack's" utmost vigilance was being exercised to keep her in the narrow channel, a boy pulled his coat-tail and hailed him with:

"Say, Mister Captain! I wish you would just stop your boat a minute—I've lost my apple overboard!"

LINCOLN'S APOLOGY TO GRANT

"General Grant is a copious worker and fighter," President Lincoln wrote to General Burnside in July, 1863, "but a meagre writer or telegrapher."

Grant never wrote a report until the battle was over.

President Lincoln wrote a letter to Grant on July 13th, 1863, which indicated the strength of the hold the successful fighter had upon the man in the White House.

It ran as follows:

"I do not remember that you and I ever met personally.

"I write this now as a grateful acknowledgment for the almost inestimable service you have done the country.

"I write to say a word further.

"When you first reached the vicinity of Vicksburg, I thought you should do what you finally did—march the troops across the neck, run the batteries with the transports, and thus go below; and I never had any faith, except a general hope, that you knew better than I, that the Yazoo Pass expedition, and the like, could succeed.

"When you got below and took Port Gibson, Grand Gulf and vicinity, I thought you should go down the river and join General Banks; and when you turned northward, east of Big Black, I feared it was a mistake.

"I now wish to make the personal acknowledgment that you were right and I was wrong."

A USELESS DOG

When Hood's army had been scattered into fragments, President Lincoln, elated by the defeat of what had so long been a menacing force on the borders of Tennessee, was reminded by its collapse of the fate of a savage dog belonging to one of his neighbors in the frontier settlements in which he lived in his youth. "The dog," he said, "was the terror of the neighborhood, and its owner, a churlish and quarrelsome fellow, took pleasure in the brute's forcible attitude.

"Finally, all other means having failed to subdue the creature, a man loaded a lump of meat with a charge of powder, to which was attached a slow fuse; this was dropped where the dreaded dog would find it, and the animal gulped down the tempting bait.

"There was a dull rumbling, a muffled explosion, and fragments of the dog were seen flying in every direction. The grieved owner, picking up the shattered remains of his cruel favorite, said: 'He was a good dog, but as a dog, his days of usefulness are over.' Hood's army was a good army," said Lincoln by way of comment, "and we were all afraid of it, but as an army, its usefulness is gone."

HE'D RUIN ALL THE OTHER CONVICTS

One of the droll stories brought into play by the President as an ally in support of his contention, proved most effective. Politics was rife among the generals of the Union Army, and there was more "wire-pulling" to prevent the advancement of fellow commanders than the laying of plans to defeat the Confederates in battle.

However, when it so happened that the name of a particularly unpopular general was sent to the Senate for confirmation, the protest against his promotion was almost unanimous. The nomination didn't seem to please anyone. Generals who were enemies before conferred together for the purpose of bringing every possible influence to bear upon the Senate and securing the rejection of the hated leader's name. The President was surprised. He had never known such unanimity before.

"You remind me," said the President to a delegation of officers which called upon him one day to present a fresh protest to him regarding the nomination, "of a visit a certain Governor paid to the Penitentiary of his State. It had been announced that the Governor would hear the story of every inmate of the institution, and was prepared to rectify, either by commutation or pardon, any wrongs that had been done to any prisoner.

"One by one the convicts appeared before His Excellency, and each one maintained that he was an innocent man, who had been sent to prison because the police didn't like him, or his friends and relatives wanted his property, or he was too popular, etc., etc. The last prisoner to appear was an individual who was not at all prepossessing. His face was against him; his eyes were shifty; he didn't have the appearance of an honest man, and he didn't act like one.

"'Well,' asked the Governor, impatiently, 'I suppose you're innocent like the rest of these fellows?'

"'No, Governor,' was the unexpected answer; 'I was guilty of the crime they charged against me, and I got just what I deserved.'

"When he had recovered from his astonishment, the Governor, looking the fellow squarely in the face, remarked with emphasis: 'I'll have to pardon you, because I don't want to leave so bad a man as you are in the company of such innocent sufferers as I have discovered your fellow-convicts to be. You might corrupt them and teach them wicked tricks. As soon as I get back to the capital, I'll have the papers made out.'

"You gentlemen," continued the President, "ought to be glad that so bad a man, as you represent this officer to be, is to get his promotion, for then you won't be forced to associate with him and suffer the contamination of his presence and influence. I will do all I can to have the Senate confirm him."

And he was confirmed.

IT WAS UP-HILL WORK

Two young men called on the President from Springfield, Illinois. Lincoln shook hands with them, and asked about the crops, the weather, etc.

Finally one of the young men said, "Mother is not well, and she sent me up to inquire of you how the suit about the Wells property is getting on."

Lincoln, in the same even tone with which he had asked the question, said: "Give my best wishes and respects to your mother, and tell her I have so many outside matters to attend to now that I have put that case, and others, in the hand of a lawyer friend of mine, and if you will call on him (giving name and address) he will give you all the information you want."

After they had gone, a friend who was present, said: "Mr. Lincoln, you did not seem to know the young men?"

He laughed and replied: "No, I had never seen them before, and I had to beat around the bush until I found who they were. It was up-hill work, but I topped it at last."

HIS "GLASS HACK"

President Lincoln had not been in the White House very long before Mrs. Lincoln became seized with the idea that a fine new barouche was about the proper thing for "the first lady in the land." The President did not care particularly about it one way or the other, and told his wife to order whatever she wanted.

Lincoln forgot all about the new vehicle, and was overcome with astonishment one afternoon when, having acceded to Mrs. Lincoln's desire to go driving, he found a beautiful barouche standing in front of the door of the White House.

His wife watched him with an amused smile, but the only remark he made was, "Well, Mary, that's about the slickest 'glass hack' in town, isn't it?"

COULD LICK ANY MAN IN THE CROWD

When the enemies of General Grant were bothering the President with emphatic and repeated demands that the "Silent Man" be removed from command, Mr. Lincoln remained firm. He would not consent to lose the services of so valuable a soldier. "Grant fights," said he in response to the charges made that Grant was a butcher, a drunkard, an incompetent and a general who did not know his business.

"That reminds me of a story," President Lincoln said one day to a delegation of the "Grant-is-no-good" style.

"Out in my State of Illinois there was a man nominated for sheriff of the county. He was a good man for the office, brave, determined and honest, but not much of an orator. In fact, he couldn't talk at all; he couldn't make a speech to save his life.

"His friends knew he was a man who would preserve the peace of the county and perform the duties devolving upon him all right, but the people of the county didn't know it. They wanted him to come out boldly on the platform at political meetings and state his convictions and principles; they had been used to speeches from candidates, and were somewhat suspicious of a man who was afraid to open his mouth.

"At last the candidate consented to make a speech, and his friends were delighted. The candidate was on hand, and, when he was called upon, advanced to the front and faced the crowd. There was a glitter in his eye that wasn't pleasing, and the way he walked out to the front of the stand showed that he knew just what he wanted to say.

"'Feller Citizens,' was his beginning, the words spoken quietly, 'I'm not a speakin' man; I ain't no orator, an' I never stood up before a lot of people in my life before; I'm not goin' to make no speech, 'xcept to say that I can lick any man in the crowd!'"

NO DEATHS IN HIS HOUSE

A gentleman was relating to the President how a friend of his had been driven away from New Orleans as a Unionist, and how, on his expulsion, when he asked to see the writ by which he was expelled, the deputation which called on him told him the Government would do nothing illegal, and so they had issued no illegal writs, and simply meant to make him go of his own free will.

"Well," said Mr. Lincoln, "that reminds me of a hotel-keeper down at St. Louis, who boasted that he never had a death in his hotel, for whenever a guest was dying in his house, he carried him out to die in the gutter."

LINCOLN'S NAME FOR "WEEPING WATER"

"I was speaking one time to Mr. Lincoln," said Governor Saunders, of Nebraska, "of a little Nebraskan settlement on the Weeping Water, a stream in our State."

"'Weeping Water!' said he.

"Then with a twinkle in his eye, he continued:

"'I suppose the Indians out there call it Minneboohoo, don't they? They ought to, if Laughing Water is Minnehaha in their language.'"

EASIER TO EMPTY THE POTOMAC

An officer of low volunteer rank persisted in telling and re-telling his troubles to the President on a summer afternoon when Lincoln was tired and careworn.

After listening patiently, he finally turned upon the broad Potomac in the distance, said in a peremptory tone that ended the interview:

"Now, my man, go away, go away. I cannot meddle in your case. I could as easily bail out the Potomac River with a teaspoon as attend to all the details of the army."

A "FREE FOR ALL"

Lincoln made a political speech at Pappsville, Illinois, when a candidate for the Legislature the first time. A free-for-all fight began soon after the opening of the meeting, and Lincoln, noticing one of his friends about to succumb to the energetic attack of an infuriated ruffian, edged his way through the crowd, and, seizing the bully by the neck and the seat of his trousers, threw him, by means of his strength and long arms, as one witness stoutly insists, "twelve feet away." Returning to the stand, and throwing aside his hat, he inaugurated his campaign with the following brief but pertinent declaration:

"Fellow-citizens, I presume you all know who I am. I am humble Abraham Lincoln. I have been solicited by many friends to become a candidate for the Legislature. My politics are short and sweet, like the old woman's dance. I am in favor of the national bank; I am in favor of the internal improvement system and a high protective tariff. These are my sentiments; if elected, I shall be thankful; if not, it will be all the same."

THE OTHER ONE WAS WORSE

It so happened that an official of the War Department had escaped serious punishment for a rather flagrant offense, by showing where grosser irregularities existed in the management of a certain Bureau of the Department. So valuable was the information furnished that the culprit who "gave the snap away" was not even discharged.

"That reminds me," the President said, when the case was laid before him, "of a story about Daniel Webster, when the latter was a boy.

"When quite young, at school, Daniel was one day guilty of a gross violation of the rules. He was detected in the act, and called up by the teacher for punishment.

"This was to be the old-fashioned 'feruling' of the hand. His hands happened to be very dirty.

"Knowing this, on the way to the teacher's desk, he spit upon the palm of his right hand, wiping it off upon the side of his pantaloons.

"'Give me your hand, sir,' said the teacher, very sternly.

"Out went the right hand, partly cleansed. The teacher looked at it a moment, and said:

"'Daniel, if you will find another hand in this school-room as filthy as that, I will let you off this time!'

"Instantly from behind his back came the left hand.

"'Here it is, sir,' was the ready reply.

"'That will do,' said the teacher, 'for this time; you can take your seat, sir.'"

COULD MAKE "RABBIT-TRACKS"

When a grocery clerk at New Salem, the annual election came around. A Mr. Graham was clerk, but his assistant was absent, and it was necessary to find a man to fill his place. Lincoln, a "tall young man," had already concentrated on himself the attention of the people of the town, and Graham easily discovered him. Asking him if he could write, "Abe" modestly replied, "I can make a few rabbit-tracks." His rabbit-tracks proving to be legible and even graceful, he was employed.

The voters soon discovered that the new assistant clerk was honest and fair, and performed his duties satisfactorily, and when, the work done, he began to "entertain them with stories," they found that their town had made a valuable personal and social acquisition.

PETER CARTWRIGHT'S DESCRIPTION OF LINCOLN

Peter Cartwright, the famous and eccentric old Methodist preacher, who used to ride a church circuit, as Mr. Lincoln and others did the court circuit, did not like Lincoln very well, probably because Mr. Lincoln was not a member of his flock and once defeated the preacher for Congress. This was Cartwright's description of Lincoln: "This Lincoln is a man six feet four inches tall, but so angular that if you should drop a plummet from the center of his head it would cut him three times before it touched his feet."

WISHED THE ARMY CHARGED LIKE THAT

A prominent volunteer officer who, early in the War, was on duty in Washington and often carried reports to Secretary Stanton at the War Department, told a characteristic story on President Lincoln. Said he:

"I was with several other young officers, also carrying reports to the War Department, and one morning we were late. In this instance we were in a desperate hurry to deliver the papers, in order to be able to catch the train returning to camp.

"On the winding, dark staircase of the old War Department, which many will remember, it was our misfortune, while taking about three stairs at a time, to run a certain head like a catapult into the body of the President, striking him in the region of the right lower vest pocket.

"The usual surprised and relaxed grunt of a man thus assailed came promptly.

"We quickly sent an apology in the direction of the dimly seen form, feeling that the ungracious shock was expensive, even to the humblest clerk in the department.

"A second glance revealed to us the President as the victim of the collision. Then followed a special tender of 'ten thousand pardons,' and the President's reply: "'One's enough; I wish the whole army would charge like that.'"

"UNCLE ABRAHAM" HAD EVERYTHING READY

"You can't do anything with them Southern fellows," the old man at the table was saying.

"If they get whipped, they'll retreat to them Southern swamps and bayous along with the fishes and crocodiles. You haven't got the fish-nets made that'll catch 'em."

"Look here, old gentleman," remarked President Lincoln, who was sitting alongside, "we've got just the nets for traitors, in the bayous or anywhere."

"Hey? What nets?"

"Bayou-nets!" and "Uncle Abraham" pointed his joke with his fork, spearing a fishball savagely.

DIDN'T TRUST THE COURT

In one of his many stories of Lincoln, his law partner, W. H. Herndon, told this as illustrating Lincoln's shrewdness as a lawyer:

"I was with Lincoln once and listened to an oral argument by him in which he rehearsed an extended history of the law. It was a carefully prepared and masterly discourse, but, as I thought, entirely useless. After he was through and we were walking home, I asked him why he went so far back in the history of the law. I presumed the court knew enough history.

"'That's where you're mistaken,' was his instant rejoinder. 'I dared not trust the case on the presumption that the court knows everything—in fact I argued it on the presumption that the court didn't know anything,' a statement, which, when one reviews the decision of our appellate courts, is not so extravagant as one would at first suppose."

"TAD" GOT HIS DOLLAR

No matter who was with the President, or how intently absorbed, his little son "Tad" was always welcome. He almost always accompanied his father.

Once, on the way to Fortress Monroe, he became very troublesome. The President was much engaged in conversation with the party who accompanied him, and he at length said:

"'Tad,' if you will be a good boy, and not disturb me any more until we get to Fortress Monroe, I will give you a dollar."

The hope of reward was effectual for a while in securing silence, but, boylike, "Tad" soon forgot his promise, and was as noisy as ever. Upon reaching their destination, however, he said, very promptly: "Father, I want my dollar." Mr. Lincoln looked at him half-reproachfully for an instant, and then, taking from his pocketbook a dollar note, he said: "Well, my son, at any rate, I will keep my part of the bargain."

ROUGH ON THE NEGRO

Mr. Lincoln, one day, was talking with the Rev. Dr. Sunderland about the Emancipation Proclamation and the future of the negro. Suddenly a ripple of amusement broke the solemn tone of his voice. "As for the negroes, Doctor, and what is going to become of them: I told Ben Wade the other day, that it made me think of a story I read in one of my first books, 'Æsop's Fables.' It was an old edition, and had curious rough wood cuts, one of which showed three white men scrubbing a negro in a potash kettle filled with cold water. The text explained that the men thought that by scrubbing the negro they might make him white. Just about the time they thought they were succeeding, he took cold and died. Now, I am afraid that by the time we get through this war the negro will catch cold and die."

"LONG ABE'S" FEET "PROTRUDED OVER"

George M. Pullman, the great sleeping car builder, once told a joke in which Lincoln was the prominent figure. In fact, there wouldn't have been any joke had it not been for "Long Abe." At the time of the occurrence, which was the foundation for the joke—and Pullman admitted that the latter was on him—Pullman was the conductor of his only sleeping-car. The latter was an experiment, and Pullman was doing everything possible to get the railroads to take hold of it.

"One night," said Pullman in telling the story, "as we were about going out of Chicago—this was long before Lincoln was what you might call a renowned man—a long, lean, ugly man, with a wart on his cheek, came into the depot. He paid me fifty cents, and half a berth was assigned him. Then he took off his coat and vest and hung them up, and they fitted the peg about as well as they fitted him. Then he kicked off his boots, which were of surprising length, turned into the berth, and, undoubtedly having an easy conscience, was sleeping like a healthy baby before the car left the depot.

"Pretty soon along came another passenger and paid his fifty cents. In two minutes he was back at me, angry as a wet hen.

"'There's a man in that berth of mine,' said he hotly, 'and he's about ten feet high. How am I going to sleep there, I'd like to know? Go and look at him.'

"In I went—mad, too. The tall, lank man's knees were under his chin, his arms were stretched across the bed and his feet were stored comfortably— for him. I shook him until he awoke, and then told him if he wanted the whole berth he would have to pay $1.

"'My dear sir,' said the tall man, 'a contract is a contract. I have paid you fifty cents for half this berth, and, as you see, I'm occupying it. There's the other half,' pointing to a strip about six inches wide. 'Sell that and don't disturb me again.'

"And so saying, the man with a wart on his face went to sleep again. He was Abraham Lincoln, and he never grew any shorter afterward. We became great friends, and often laughed over the incident."

"I'D A BEEN MISSED BY MYSE'F"

The President did not consider that every soldier who ran away in battle, or did not stand firmly to receive a bayonet charge, was a coward. He was of opinion that self-preservation was the first law of Nature, but he didn't want this statute construed too liberally by the troops.

At the same time he took occasion to illustrate a point he wished to make by a story in connection with a darky who was a member of the Ninth Illinois Infantry Regiment. This regiment was one of those engaged at the capture of Fort Donelson. It behaved gallantly, and lost as heavily as any.

"Upon the hurricane-deck of one of our gunboats," said the President in telling the story, "I saw an elderly darky, with a very philosophical and retrospective cast of countenance, squatted upon his bundle, toasting his shins against the chimney, and apparently plunged into a state of profound meditation.

"As the negro rather interested me, I made some inquiries, and found that he had really been with the Ninth Illinois Infantry at Donelson, and began to ask him some questions about the capture of the place.

"'Were you in the fight?' "'Had a little taste of it, sa.'

"'Stood your ground, did you?' "'No, sa, I runs.'

"'Run at the first fire, did you?'

"'Yes, sa, and would hab run soona, had I knowd it war comin'.' "'Why, that wasn't very creditable to your courage.'

"'Dat isn't in my line, sa—cookin's my profeshun.' "'Well, but have you no regard for your reputation?' "'Reputation's nuffin to me by de side ob life.'

"'Do you consider your life worth more than other people's?' "'It's worth more to me, sa.'

"'Then you must value it very highly?'

"'Yes, sa, I does, more dan all dis wuld, more dan a million ob dollars, sa, for what would dat be wuth to a man wid de bref out ob him? Self- preserbation am de fust law wid me.'

"'But why should you act upon a different rule from other men?'

"'Different men set different values on their lives; mine is not in de market.'

"'But if you lost it you would have the satisfaction of knowing that you died for your country.'

"'Dat no satisfaction when feelin's gone.'

"'Then patriotism and honor are nothing to you?'

"'Nufin whatever, sa—I regard them as among the vanities.'

"'If our soldiers were like you, traitors might have broken up the government without resistance.'

"'Yes, sa, dar would hab been no help for it. I wouldn't put my life in de scale 'g'inst any gobernment dat eber existed, for no gobernment could replace de loss to me.'

"'Do you think any of your company would have missed you if you had been killed?'

"'Maybe not, sa; a dead white man ain't much to dese sojers, let alone a dead nigga—but I'd a missed myse'f, and dat was de p'int wid me.'

"I only tell this story," concluded the President, "in order to illustrate the result of the tactics of some of the Union generals who would be sadly 'missed' by themselves, if by no one else, if they ever got out of the Army."

LOST HIS CERTIFICATE OF CHARACTER

Mr. Lincoln prepared his first inaugural address in a room over a store in Springfield. His only reference works were Henry Clay's great compromise speech of 1850, Andrew Jackson's Proclamation against Nullification, Webster's great reply to Hayne, and a copy of the Constitution.

When Mr. Lincoln started for Washington, to be inaugurated, the inaugural address was placed in a special satchel and guarded with special care. At Harrisburg the satchel was given in charge of Robert T. Lincoln, who accompanied his father. Before the train started from Harrisburg the precious satchel was missing. Robert thought he had given it to a waiter at the hotel, but a long search failed to reveal the missing satchel with its precious document. Lincoln was annoyed, angry, and finally in despair. He felt certain that the address was lost beyond recovery, and, as it lacked only ten days until the inauguration, he had no time to prepare another. He had not even preserved the notes from which the original copy had been written.

Mr. Lincoln went to Ward Lamon, his former law partner, then one of his body-guards, and informed him of the loss in the following words:

"Lamon, I guess I have lost my certificate of moral character, written by myself. Bob has lost my gripsack containing my inaugural address."

Of course the misfortune reminded him of a story.

"I feel," said Mr. Lincoln, "a good deal as the old member of the Methodist Church did when he lost his wife at the camp meeting, and went up to an old elder of the church and asked him if he could tell him whereabouts in h

—l his wife was. In fact, I am in a worse fix than my Methodist friend, for if it were only a wife that were missing, mine would be sure to bob up somewhere."

The clerk at the hotel told Mr. Lincoln that he would probably find his missing satchel in the baggage-room. Arriving there, Mr. Lincoln saw a satchel which he thought was his, and it was passed out to him. His key fitted the lock, but alas! when it was opened the satchel contained only a soiled shirt, some paper collars, a pack of cards and a bottle of whisky. A few minutes later the satchel containing the inaugural address was found among the pile of baggage.

The recovery of the address also reminded Mr. Lincoln of a story, which is thus narrated by Ward Lamon in his "Recollections of Abraham Lincoln":

The loss of the address and the search for it was the subject of a great deal of amusement. Mr. Lincoln said many funny things in connection with the incident. One of them was that he knew a fellow once who had saved up fifteen hundred dollars, and had placed it in a private banking establishment. The bank soon failed, and he afterward received ten per cent of his investment. He then took his one hundred and fifty dollars and deposited it in a savings bank, where he was sure it would be safe. In a short time this bank also failed, and he received at the final settlement ten per cent on the amount deposited. When the fifteen dollars was paid over to him, he held it in his hand and looked at it thoughtfully; then he said, "Now, darn you, I have got you reduced to a portable shape, so I'll put you in my pocket." Suiting the action to the word, Mr. Lincoln took his address from the bag and carefully placed it in the inside pocket of his vest, but held on to the satchel with as much interest as if it still contained his "certificate of moral character."

THE CASE OF BETSY ANN DOUGHERTY

Many requests and petitions made to Mr. Lincoln when he was President were ludicrous and trifling, but he always entered into them with that humor-loving spirit that was such a relief from the grave duties of his great office.

Once a party of Southerners called on him in behalf of one Betsy Ann Dougherty. The spokesman, who was an ex-governor, said:

"Mr. President, Betsy Ann Dougherty is a good woman. She lived in my county and did my washing for a long time. Her husband went off and joined the rebel army, and I wish you would give her a protection paper." The solemnity of this appeal struck Mr. Lincoln as uncommonly ridiculous.

The two men looked at each other—the Governor desperately in earnest, and the President masking his humor behind the gravest exterior. At last Mr. Lincoln asked, with inimitable gravity, "Was Betsy Ann a good washerwoman?" "Oh, yes, sir, she was, indeed."

"Was your Betsy Ann an obliging woman?" "Yes, she was certainly very kind," responded the Governor, soberly.

"Could she do other things than wash?" continued Mr. Lincoln with the same portentous gravity.

"Oh, yes; she was very kind—very."

"Where is Betsy Ann?"

"She is now in New York, and wants to come back to Missouri, but she is afraid of banishment."

"Is anybody meddling with her?"

"No; but she is afraid to come back unless you will give her a protection paper."

Thereupon Mr. Lincoln wrote on a visiting card the following:

"Let Betsy Ann Dougherty alone as long as she behaves herself. "A. LINCOLN."

He handed this card to her advocate, saying, "Give this to Betsy Ann."

"But, Mr. President, couldn't you write a few words to the officers that would insure her protection?"

"No," said Mr. Lincoln, "officers have no time now to read letters. Tell Betsy Ann to put a string in this card and hang it around her neck. When the officers see this, they will keep their hands off your Betsy Ann."

"FOOLING" THE PEOPLE

Lincoln was a strong believer in the virtue of dealing honestly with the people.

"If you once forfeit the confidence of your fellow-citizens," he said to a caller at the White House, "you can never regain their respect and esteem.

"It is true that you may fool all the people some of the time; you can even fool some of the people all the time; but you can't fool all of the people all the time."

HER ONLY IMPERFECTION

At one time a certain Major Hill charged Lincoln with making defamatory remarks regarding Mrs. Hill.

Hill was insulting in his language to Lincoln, who never lost his temper.

When he saw his chance to edge a word in, Lincoln denied emphatically using the language or anything like that attributed to him.

He entertained, he insisted, a high regard for Mrs. Hill, and the only thing he knew to her discredit was the fact that she was Major Hill's wife.

HE "BROKE" TO WIN

A lawyer, who was a stranger to Mr. Lincoln, once expressed to General Linder the opinion that Mr. Lincoln's practice of telling stories to the jury was a waste of time.

"Don't lay that flattering unction to your soul," Linder answered; "Lincoln is like Tansey's horse, he 'breaks to win.'"

"BAP." MCNABB'S ROOSTER

It is true that Lincoln did not drink, never swore, was a stranger to smoking and lived a moral life generally, but he did like horse-racing and chicken fighting. New Salem, Illinois, where Lincoln was "clerking," was known the neighborhood around as a "fast" town, and the average young man made no very desperate resistance when tempted to join in the drinking and gambling bouts.

"Bap." McNabb was famous for his ability in both the raising and the purchase of roosters of prime fighting quality, and when his birds fought the attendance was large. It was because of the "flunking" of one of "Bap.'s" roosters that Lincoln was enabled to make a point when criticising McClellan's unreadiness and lack of energy.

One night there was a fight on the schedule, one of "Bap." McNabb's birds being a contestant. "Bap." brought a little red rooster, whose fighting qualities had been well advertised for days in advance, and much interest was manifested in the outcome. As the result of these contests was generally a quarrel, in which each man, charging foul play, seized his victim, they chose Lincoln umpire, relying not only on his fairness but his ability to enforce his decisions. Judge Herndon, in his "Abraham Lincoln," says of this notable event:

"I cannot improve on the description furnished me in February, 1865, by one who was present.

"They formed a ring, and the time having arrived, Lincoln, with one hand on each hip and in a squatting position, cried, 'Ready.' Into the ring they toss their fowls, 'Bap.'s' red rooster along with the rest. But no sooner had the little beauty discovered what was to be done than he dropped his tail and ran.

"The crowd cheered, while 'Bap.' in disappointment, picked him up and started away, losing his quarter (entrance fee) and carrying home his dishonored fowl. Once arrived at the latter place he threw his pet down with a feeling of indignation and chagrin.

"The little fellow, out of sight of all rivals, mounted a woodpile and proudly flirting out his feathers, crowed with all his might. 'Bap.' looked on in disgust.

"'Yes, you little cuss,' he exclaimed, irreverently, 'you're great on dress parade, but not worth a darn in a fight.'"

It is said, according to Judge Herndon, that Lincoln considered McClellan as "great on dress parade," but not so much in a fight.

LINCOLN'S FIRST SPEECH

Lincoln made his first speech when he was a mere boy, going barefoot, his trousers held up by one suspender, and his shock of hair sticking through a hole in the crown of his cheap straw hat.

"Abe," in company with Dennis Hanks, attended a political meeting, which was addressed by a typical stump speaker—one of those loud-voiced fellows who shouted at the top of his voice, and waved his arms wildly.

At the conclusion of the speech, which did not meet the views either of "Abe" or Dennis, the latter declared that "Abe" could make a better speech than that. Whereupon he got a dry-goods box and called on "Abe" to reply to the campaign orator.

Lincoln threw his old straw hat on the ground, and, mounting the dry-goods box, delivered a speech which held the attention of the crowd and won him considerable applause. Even the campaign orator admitted that it was a fine speech and answered every point in his own "oration."

Dennis Hanks, who thought "Abe" was about the greatest man that ever lived, was delighted, and he often told how young "Abe" got the better of the trained campaign speaker.

TOO MANY PIGS FOR THE TEATS

An applicant for a sutlership in the army relates this story: "In the winter of 1864, after serving three years in the Union Army, and being honorably discharged, I made application for the post sutlership at Point Lookout. My father being interested, we made application to Mr. Stanton, the Secretary of War. We obtained an audience, and were ushered into the presence of the most pompous man I ever met. As I entered he waved his hand for me to stop at a given distance from him, and then he put these questions, viz.:

"'Did you serve three years in the army?' "'I

did sir.'

"'Were you honorably discharged?' "'I

was, sir.'

"'Let me see your discharge.'

"I gave it to him. He looked it over, then said: 'Were you ever wounded?' I told him yes, at the battle of Williamsburg, May 5, 1861.

"He then said: 'I think we can give this position to a soldier who has lost an arm or leg, he being more deserving;' and he then said I looked hearty and healthy enough to serve three years more. He would not give me a chance to argue my case.

"The audience was at an end. He waved his hand to me. I was then dismissed from the august presence of the Honorable Secretary of War.

"My father was waiting for me in the hallway, who saw by my countenance that I was not successful. I said to my father:

"'Let us go over to Mr. Lincoln; he may give us more satisfaction.'

"He said it would do me no good, but we went over. Mr. Lincoln's reception room was full of ladies and gentlemen when we entered.

"My turn soon came. Lincoln turned to my father and said:

"'Now, gentlemen, be pleased to be as quick as possible with your business, as it is growing late.'

"My father then stepped up to Lincoln and introduced me to him. Lincoln then said:

"'Take a seat, gentlemen, and state your business as quickly as possible.'

"There was but one chair by Lincoln, so he motioned my father to sit, while I stood. My father stated the business to him as stated above. He then said:

"'Have you seen Mr. Stanton?'

"We told him yes, that he had refused. He (Mr. Lincoln) then said:

"'Gentlemen, this is Mr. Stanton's business; I cannot interfere with him; he attends to all these matters and I am sorry I cannot help you.'

"He saw that we were disappointed, and did his best to revive our spirits. He succeeded well with my father, who was a Lincoln man, and who was a staunch Republican.

"Mr. Lincoln then said:

"'Now, gentlemen, I will tell you what it is; I have thousands of applications like this every day, but we cannot satisfy all for this reason, that these positions are like office seekers—there are too many pigs for the teats.'

"The ladies who were listening to the conversation placed their handkerchiefs to their faces and turned away. But the joke of 'Old Abe' put us all in a good humor. We then left the presence of the greatest and most just man who ever lived to fill the Presidential chair."

MORE PEGS THAN HOLES

Some gentlemen were once finding fault with the President because certain generals were not given commands.

"The fact is," replied President Lincoln, "I have got more pegs than I have holes to put them in."

FEW, BUT BOISTEROUS

Lincoln was a very quiet man, and went about his business in a quiet way, making the least noise possible. He heartily disliked those boisterous people who were constantly deluging him with advice, and shouting at the tops of their voices whenever they appeared at the White House. "These noisy people create a great clamor," said he one day, in conversation with some personal friends, "and remind me, by the way, of a good story I heard out in Illinois while I was practicing, or trying to practice, some law there. I will say, though, that I practiced more law than I ever got paid for.

"A fellow who lived just out of town, on the bank of a large marsh, conceived a big idea in the money-making line. He took it to a prominent merchant, and began to develop his plans and specifications. 'There are at least ten million frogs in that marsh near me, an' I'll just arrest a couple of carloads of them and hand them over to you. You can send them to the big cities and make lots of money for both of us. Frogs' legs are great delicacies in the big towns, an' not very plentiful. It won't take me more'n two or three days to pick 'em. They make so much noise my family can't sleep, and by this deal, I'll get rid of a nuisance and gather in some cash.'

"The merchant agreed to the proposition, promised the fellow he would pay him well for the two carloads. Two days passed, then three, and finally two weeks were gone before the fellow showed up again, carrying a small basket. He looked weary and 'done up,' and he wasn't talkative a bit. He threw the basket on the counter with the remark, 'There's your frogs.'

"'You haven't two carloads in that basket, have you?' inquired the merchant. "'No,' was the reply, 'and there ain't two carloads in this blasted world.'

"'I thought you said there were at least ten millions of 'em in that marsh near you, according to the noise they made,' observed the merchant. 'Your people couldn't sleep because of 'em.'

"'Well,' said the fellow, 'accordin' to the noise they made, there was, I thought, a hundred million of 'em, but when I had waded and swum that there marsh day and night for two blessed weeks, I couldn't harvest but six. There's two or three left yet, an' the marsh is as noisy as it uster be. We haven't catched up on any of our lost sleep yet. Now, you can have these here six, an' I won't charge you a cent fer 'em.'

"You can see by this little yarn," remarked the President, "that these boisterous people make too much noise in proportion to their numbers."

THE PRESIDENTIAL "CHIN-FLY"

Some of Mr. Lincoln's intimate friends once called his attention to a certain member of his Cabinet who was quietly working to secure a nomination for the Presidency, although knowing that Mr. Lincoln was to be a candidate for re-election. His friends insisted that the Cabinet officer ought to be made to give up his Presidential aspirations or be removed from office. The situation reminded Mr. Lincoln of a story: "My brother and I," he said, "were once plowing corn, I driving the horse and he holding the plow. The horse was lazy, but on one occasion he rushed across the field so that I, with my long legs, could scarcely keep pace with him. On reaching the end of the furrow, I found an enormous chin-fly fastened upon him, and knocked him off. My brother asked me what I did that for. I told him I didn't want the old horse bitten in that way. 'Why,' said my brother, 'that's all that made him go.' Now," said Mr. Lincoln, "if Mr. —— has a Presidential chin-fly biting him, I'm not going to knock him off, if it will only make his department go."

"WEBSTER COULDN'T HAVE DONE MORE"

Lincoln "got even" with the Illinois Central Railroad Company, in 1855, in a most substantial way, at the same time secured sweet revenge for an insult, unwarranted in every way, put upon him by one of the officials of that corporation.

Lincoln and Herndon defended the Illinois Central Railroad in an action brought by McLean County, Illinois, in August, 1853, to recover taxes alleged to be due the county from the road. The Legislature had granted the road immunity from taxation, and this was a case intended to test the constitutionality of the law. The road sent a retainer fee of $250.

In the lower court the case was decided in favor of the railroad. An appeal to the Supreme Court followed, was argued twice, and finally decided in favor of the road. This last decision was rendered some time in 1855. Lincoln then went to Chicago, and presented the bill for legal services. Lincoln and Herndon only asked for $2,000 more.

The official to whom he was referred, after looking at the bill, expressed great surprise.

"Why, sir," he exclaimed, "this is as much as Daniel Webster himself would have charged. We cannot allow such a claim."

"Why not?" asked Lincoln.

"We could have hired first-class lawyers at that figure," was the response.

"We won the case, didn't we?" queried Lincoln.

"Certainly," replied the official.

"Daniel Webster, then," retorted Lincoln in no amiable tone, "couldn't have done more," and "Abe" walked out of the official's office.

Lincoln withdrew the bill, and started for home. On the way he stopped at Bloomington, where he met Grant Goodrich, Archibald Williams, Norman B. Judd, O. H. Browning, and other attorneys, who, on learning of his modest charge for the valuable services rendered the railroad, induced him to increase the demand to $5,000, and to bring suit for that sum.

This was done at once. On the trial six lawyers certified that the bill was reasonable, and judgment for that sum went by default; the judgment was promptly paid, and, of course, his partner, Herndon, got "your half, Billy" without delay.

LONG AND SHORT OF IT

On the occasion of a serenade, the President was called for by the crowd assembled. He appeared at a window with his wife (who was somewhat below the medium height), and made the following "brief remarks":

"Here I am, and here is Mrs. Lincoln. That's the long and the short of it."

'SQUIRE BAGLY'S PRECEDENT

Mr. T. W. S. Kidd, of Springfield, says that he once heard a lawyer opposed to Lincoln trying to convince a jury that precedent was superior to law, and that custom made things legal in all cases. When Lincoln arose to answer him he told the jury he would argue his case in the same way.

"Old 'Squire Bagly, from Menard, came into my office and said, 'Lincoln, I want your advice as a lawyer. Has a man what's been elected justice of the peace a right to issue a marriage license?' I told him he had not; when the old 'squire threw himself back in his chair very indignantly, and said, 'Lincoln, I thought you was a lawyer. Now Bob Thomas and me had a bet on this thing, and we agreed to let you decide; but if this is your opinion I don't want it, for I know a thunderin' sight better, for I have been 'squire now for eight years and have done it all the time.'"

TOM CORWIN'S LATEST STORY

One of Mr. Lincoln's warm friends was Dr. Robert Boal, of Lacon, Illinois. Telling of a visit he paid to the White House soon after Mr. Lincoln's inauguration, he said: "I found him the same Lincoln as a struggling lawyer and politician that I did in Washington as President of the United States, yet there was a dignity and self-possession about him in his high official authority. I paid him a second call in the evening. He had thrown off his reserve somewhat, and would walk up and down the room with his hands to his sides and laugh at the joke he was telling, or at one that was told to him. I remember one story he told to me on this occasion.

"Tom Corwin, of Ohio, had been down to Alexandria, Va., that day and had come back and told Lincoln a story which pleased him so much that he broke out in a hearty laugh and said: 'I must tell you Tom Corwin's latest.

Tom met an old man at Alexandria who knew George Washington, and he told Tom that George Washington often swore. Now, Corwin's father had always held the father of our country up as a faultless person and told his son to follow in his footsteps.

""Well," said Corwin, "when I heard that George Washington was addicted to the vices and infirmities of man, I felt so relieved that I just shouted for joy."'"

THE CABINET WAS A-SETTIN'

Being in Washington one day, the Rev. Robert Collyer thought he'd take a look around. In passing through the grounds surrounding the White House, he cast a glance toward the Presidential residence, and was astonished to see three pairs of feet resting on the ledge of an open window in one of the apartments of the second story. The divine paused for a moment, calmly surveyed the unique spectacle, and then resumed his walk toward the War Department. Seeing a laborer at work not far from the Executive Mansion, Mr. Collyer asked him what it all meant. To whom, did the feet belong, and particularly, the mammoth ones? "You old fool," answered the workman, "that's the Cabinet, which is a-settin', an' them thar big feet belongs to 'Old Abe.'"

"MASSA LINKUM LIKE DE LORD!"

By the Act of Emancipation President Lincoln built for himself forever the first place in the affections of the African race in this country. The love and reverence manifested for him by many of these people has, on some occasions, almost reached adoration. One day, Colonel McKaye, of New York, who had been one of a committee to investigate the condition of the freedmen, upon his return from Hilton Head and Beaufort called upon the President, and in the course of the interview said that up to the time of the arrival among them in the South of the Union forces they had no knowledge of any other power. Their masters fled upon the approach of our soldiers, and this gave the slaves the conception of a power greater than their masters exercised. This power they called "Massa Linkum."

Colonel McKaye said their place of worship was a large building they called "the praise house," and the leader of the "meeting," a venerable black man, was known as "the praise man."

On a certain day, when there was quite a large gathering of the people, considerable confusion was created by different persons attempting to tell who and what "Massa Linkum" was. In the midst of the excitement the white-headed leader commanded silence. "Brederen," said he, "you don't know nosen' what you'se talkin' 'bout. Now, you just listen to me. Massa Linkum, he ebery whar. He know ebery ting."

Then, solemnly looking up, he added: "He walk de earf like de Lord!"

A BULLET THROUGH HIS HAT

A soldier tells the following story of an attempt upon the life of Mr. Lincoln:

"One night I was doing sentinel duty at the entrance to the Soldiers' Home. This was about the middle of August, 1864. About eleven o'clock I heard a rifle shot, in the direction of the city, and shortly afterwards I heard approaching hoof-beats. In two or three minutes a horse came dashing up. I recognized the belated President. The President was bare-headed. The President simply thought his horse had taken fright at the discharge of the firearms.

"On going back to the place where the shot had been heard, we found the President's hat. It was a plain silk hat, and upon examination we discovered a bullet hole through the crown.

"The next day, upon receiving the hat, the President remarked that it was made by some foolish marksman, and was not intended for him; but added that he wished nothing said about the matter.

"The President said, philosophically: 'I long ago made up my mind that if anybody wants to kill me, he will do it. Besides, in this case, it seems to me, the man who would succeed me would be just as objectionable to my enemies—if I have any.'

"One dark night, as he was going out with a friend, he took along a heavy cane, remarking, good-naturedly:

"'Mother (Mrs. Lincoln) has got a notion into her head that I shall be assassinated, and to please her I take a cane when I go over to the War Department at night—when I don't forget it.'"

THE GENERAL WAS "HEADED IN"

A Union general, operating with his command in West Virginia, allowed himself and his men to be trapped, and it was feared his force would be captured by the Confederates. The President heard the report read by the operator, as it came over the wire, and remarked:

"Once there was a man out West who was 'heading' a barrel, as they used to call it. He worked like a good fellow in driving down the hoops, but just about the time he thought he had the job done, the head would fall in. Then he had to do the work all over again.

"All at once a bright idea entered his brain, and he wondered how it was he hadn't figured it out before. His boy, a bright, smart lad, was standing by, very much interested in the business, and, lifting the young one up, he put him inside the barrel, telling him to hold the head in its proper place, while he pounded down the hoops on the sides. This worked like a charm, and he soon had the 'heading' done.

"Then he realized that his boy was inside the barrel, and how to get him out he couldn't for his life figure out. General Blank is now inside the barrel, 'headed in,' and the job now is to get him out."

"MIXING" AND "MINGLING"

An Eastern newspaper writer told how Lincoln, after his first nomination, received callers, the majority of them at his law office:

"While talking to two or three gentlemen and standing up, a very hard looking customer rolled in and tumbled into the only vacant chair and the one lately occupied by Mr. Lincoln. Mr. Lincoln's keen eye took in the fact, but gave no evidence of the notice.

"Turning around at last he spoke to the odd specimen, holding out his hand at such a distance that our friend had to vacate the chair if he accepted the proffered shake. Mr. Lincoln quietly resumed his chair.

"It was a small matter, yet one giving proof more positively than a larger event of that peculiar way the man has of mingling with a mixed crowd."

WANTED TO BURN HIM DOWN TO THE STUMP

Preston King once introduced A. J. Bleeker to the President, and the latter, being an applicant for office, was about to hand Mr. Lincoln his vouchers, when he was asked to read them. Bleeker had not read very far when the President disconcerted him by the exclamation, "Stop a minute! You remind me exactly of the man who killed the dog; in fact, you are just like him."

"In what respect?" asked Bleeker, not feeling he had received a compliment.

"Well," replied the President, "this man had made up his mind to kill his dog, an ugly brute, and proceeded to knock out his brains with a club. He continued striking the dog after the latter was dead until a friend protested, exclaiming, 'You needn't strike him any more; the dog is dead; you killed him at the first blow.'

"'Oh, yes,' said he, 'I know that; but I believe in punishment after death.' So, I see, do you."

Bleeker acknowledged it was possible to overdo a good thing, and then came back at the President with an anecdote of a good priest who converted an Indian from heathenism to Christianity; the only difficulty he had with him was to get him to pray for his enemies. "This Indian had been taught to over-come and destroy all his friends he didn't like," said Bleeker, "but the priest told him that while that might be the Indian method, it was not the doctrine of Christianity of the Bible. 'Saint Paul distinctly says,' the priest told him, 'If thine enemy hunger, feed him; if he thirst, give him drink.'

"The Indian shook his head at this, but when the priest added, 'For in so doing thou shalt heap coals of fire on his head,' Poor Lo was overcome with emotion, fell on his knees, and with outstretched hands and uplifted eyes invoked all sorts of blessings on the heads of all his enemies, supplicating for pleasant hunting-grounds, a large supply of squaws, lots of pappooses and all other Indian comforts.

"Finally the good priest interrupted him (as you did me, Mr. President), exclaiming, 'Stop, my son! You have discharged your Christian duty, and have done more than enough.'

"'Oh, no, father,' replied the Indian; 'let me pray. I want to burn him down to the stump!'"

CHALLENGED ALL COMERS

Personal encounters were of frequent occurrence in Gentryville in early days, and the prestige of having thrashed an opponent gave the victor marked social distinction. Green B. Taylor, with whom "Abe" worked the greater part of one winter on a farm, furnished an account of the noted fight between John Johnston, "Abe's" step-brother, and William Grigsby, in which stirring drama "Abe" himself played an important role before the curtain was rung down.

Taylor's father was the second for Johnston, and William Whitten officiated in a similar capacity for Grigsby. "They had a terrible fight," related Taylor, "and it soon became apparent that Grigsby was too much for Lincoln's man, Johnston. After they had fought a long time without interference, it having been agreed not to break the ring, 'Abe' burst through, caught Grigsby, threw him off and some feet away. There Grigsby stood, proud as Lucifer, and, swinging a bottle of liquor over his head, swore he was 'the big buck of the lick.'

"'If any one doubts it,' he shouted, 'he has only to come on and whet his horns.'"

A general engagement followed this challenge, but at the end of hostilities the field was cleared and the wounded retired amid the exultant shouts of their victors.

WITHDREW THE COLT

Mr. Alcott, of Elgin, Ill., tells of seeing Mr. Lincoln coming away from church unusually early one Sunday morning. "The sermon could not have been more than half way through," says Mr. Alcott. "'Tad' was hung across his left arm like a pair of saddle bags, and Mr. Lincoln was striding along with long, deliberate steps toward his home. On one of the street corners he encountered a group of his fellow-townsmen. Mr. Lincoln anticipated the question which was about to be put by the group, and, taking his figure of speech from practices with which they were only too familiar, said:

'Gentlemen, I entered this colt, but he kicked around so I had to withdraw him.'"

SWEET, BUT MILD REVENGE

When the United States found that a war with Black Hawk could not be dodged, Governor Reynolds, of Illinois, issued a call for volunteers, and among the companies that immediately responded was one from Menard County, Illinois. Many of these volunteers were from New Salem and Clary's Grove, and Lincoln, being out of business, was the first to enlist.

The company being full, the men held a meeting at Richland for the election of officers. Lincoln had won many hearts, and they told him that he must be their captain. It was an office to which he did not aspire, and for which he felt he had no special fitness; but he finally consented to be a candidate.

There was but one other candidate, a Mr. Kirkpatrick, who was one of the most influential men of the region. Previously, Kirkpatrick had been an employer of Lincoln, and was so overbearing in his treatment of the young man that the latter left him.

The simple mode of electing a captain adopted by the company was by placing the candidates apart, and telling the men to go and stand with the one they preferred. Lincoln and his competitor took their positions, and then the word was given. At least three out of every four went to Lincoln at once.

When it was seen by those who had arranged themselves with the other candidate that Lincoln was the choice of the majority of the company, they left their places, one by one, and came over to the successful side, until Lincoln's opponent in the friendly strife was left standing almost alone.

"I felt badly to see him cut so," says a witness of the scene.

Here was an opportunity for revenge. The humble laborer was his employer's captain, but the opportunity was never improved. Mr. Lincoln frequently confessed that no subsequent success of his life had given him half the satisfaction that this election did.

"CATCH 'EM AND CHEAT 'EM"

The lawyers on the circuit traveled by Lincoln got together one night and tried him on the charge of accepting fees which tended to lower the established rates. It was the understood rule that a lawyer should accept all the client could be induced to pay. The tribunal was known as "The Ogmathorial Court."

Ward Lamon, his law partner at the time, tells about it:

"Lincoln was found guilty and fined for his awful crime against the pockets of his brethren of the bar. The fine he paid with great good humor, and then kept the crowd of lawyers in uproarious laughter until after midnight.

"He persisted in his revolt, however, declaring that with his consent his firm should never during its life, or after its dissolution, deserve the reputation enjoyed by those shining lights of the profession, 'Catch 'em and Cheat 'em.'"

A JURYMAN'S SCORN

Lincoln had assisted in the prosecution of a man who had robbed his neighbor's hen roosts. Jogging home along the highway with the foreman of the jury that had convicted the hen stealer, he was complimented by Lincoln on the zeal and ability of the prosecution, and remarked: "Why, when the country was young, and I was stronger than I am now, I didn't mind packing off a sheep now and again, but stealing hens!" The good man's scorn could not find words to express his opinion of a man who would steal hens.

"TAD" INTRODUCES "OUR FRIENDS"

President Lincoln often avoided interviews with delegations representing various States, especially when he knew the objects of their errands, and was aware he could not grant their requests. This was the case with several commissioners from Kentucky, who were put off from day to day.

They were about to give up in despair, and were leaving the White House lobby, their speech being interspersed with vehement and uncomplimentary terms concerning "Old Abe," when "Tad" happened along. He caught at these words, and asked one of them if they wanted to see "Old Abe," laughing at the same time.

"Yes," he replied.

"Wait a minute," said "Tad," and rushed into his father's office. Said he, "Papa, may I introduce some friends to you?"

His father, always indulgent and ready to make him happy, kindly said, "Yes, my son, I will see your friends."

"Tad" went to the Kentuckians again, and asked a very dignified looking gentleman of the party his name. He was told his name. He then said, "Come, gentlemen," and they followed him.

Leading them up to the President, "Tad," with much dignity, said, "Papa, let me introduce to you Judge — —, of Kentucky;" and quickly added, "Now, Judge, you introduce the other gentlemen."

The introductions were gone through with, and they turned out to be the gentlemen Mr. Lincoln had been avoiding for a week. Mr. Lincoln reached for the boy, took him in his lap, kissed him, and told him it was all right, and that he had introduced his friend like a little gentleman as he was. Tad was eleven years old at this time.

The President was pleased with Tad's diplomacy, and often laughed at the incident as he told others of it. One day while caressing the boy, he asked him why he called those gentlemen "his friends." "Well," said Tad, "I had seen them so often, and they looked so good and sorry, and said they were from Kentucky, that I thought they must be our friends." "That is right, my son," said Mr. Lincoln; "I would have the whole human race your friends and mine, if it were possible."

STOOD UP THE LONGEST

There was a rough gallantry among the young people; and Lincoln's old comrades and friends in Indiana have left many tales of how he "went to see the girls;" of how he brought in the biggest back-log and made the brightest fire; of how the young people, sitting around it, watching the way the sparks flew, told their fortunes.

He helped pare apples, shell corn and crack nuts. He took the girls to meeting and to spelling school, though he was not often allowed to take part in the spelling-match, for the one who "chose first" always chose "Abe" Lincoln, and that was equivalent to winning, as the others knew that "he would stand up the longest."

ADMIRED THE STRONG MAN

Governor Hoyt of Wisconsin tells a story of Mr. Lincoln's great admiration for physical strength. Mr. Lincoln, in 1859, made a speech at the Wisconsin State Agricultural Fair. After the speech, in company with the Governor, he strolled about the grounds, looking at the exhibits. They came to a place where a professional "strong man" was tossing cannon balls in the air and catching them on his arms and juggling with them as though they were as light as baseballs. Mr. Lincoln had never before seen such an exhibition, and he was greatly surprised and interested.

When the performance was over, Governor Hoyt, seeing Mr. Lincoln's interest, asked him to go up and be introduced to the athlete. He did so, and, as he stood looking down musingly on the man, who was very short, and evidently wondering that one so much smaller than he could be so much stronger, he suddenly broke out with one of his quaint speeches. "Why," he said, "why, I could lick salt off the top of your hat."

SAVED LINCOLN'S LIFE

When Mr. Lincoln was quite a small boy he met with an accident that almost cost him his life. He was saved by Austin Gollaher, a young playmate. Mr. Gollaher lived to be more than ninety years of age, and to the day of his death related with great pride his boyhood association with Lincoln.

"Yes," Mr. Gollaher once said, "the story that I once saved Abraham Lincoln's life is true. He and I had been going to school together for a year or more, and had become greatly attached to each other. Then school disbanded on account of there being so few scholars, and we did not see each other much for a long while.

"One Sunday my mother visited the Lincolns, and I was taken along. 'Abe' and I played around all day. Finally, we concluded to cross the creek to hunt for some partridges young Lincoln had seen the day before. The creek was swollen by a recent rain, and, in crossing on the narrow footlog, 'Abe' fell in. Neither of us could swim. I got a long pole and held it out to 'Abe,' who grabbed it. Then I pulled him ashore.

"He was almost dead, and I was badly scared. I rolled and pounded him in good earnest. Then I got him by the arms and shook him, the water meanwhile pouring out of his mouth. By this means I succeeded in bringing him to, and he was soon all right.

"Then a new difficulty confronted us. If our mothers discovered our wet clothes they would whip us. This we dreaded from experience, and determined to avoid. It was June, the sun was very warm, and we soon dried our clothing by spreading it on the rocks about us. We promised never to tell the story, and I never did until after Lincoln's tragic end."

WOULD BLOW THEM TO H.

Mr. Lincoln had advised Lieutenant-General Winfield Scott, commanding the United States Army, of the threats of violence on inauguration day, 1861. General Scott was sick in bed at Washington when Adjutant-General Thomas Mather, of Illinois, called upon him in President-elect Lincoln's behalf, and the veteran commander was much wrought up. Said he to General Mather:

"Present my compliments to Mr. Lincoln when you return to Springfield, and tell him I expect him to come on to Washington as soon as he is ready; say to him that I will look after those Maryland and Virginia rangers myself. I will plant cannon at both ends of Pennsylvania Avenue, and if any of them show their heads or raise a finger, I'll blow them to h— —."

"I CAN STAND IT IF THEY CAN"

United States Senator Benjamin Wade, of Ohio, Henry Winter Davis, of Maryland, and Wendell Phillips were strongly opposed to President Lincoln's re-election, and Wade and Davis issued a manifesto. Phillips made several warm speeches against Lincoln and his policy.

When asked if he had read the manifesto or any of Phillips' speeches, the President replied:

"I have not seen them, nor do I care to see them. I have seen enough to satisfy me that I am a failure, not only in the opinion of the people in rebellion, but of many distinguished politicians of my own party. But time will show whether I am right or they are right, and I am content to abide its decision.

"I have enough to look after without giving much of my time to the consideration of the subject of who shall be my successor in office. The position is not an easy one, and the occupant, whoever he may be, for the next four years, will have little leisure to pluck a thorn or plant a rose in his own pathway."

It was urged that this opposition must be embarrassing to his Administration, as well as damaging to the party. He replied: "Yes, that is true; but our friends, Wade, Davis, Phillips, and others are hard to please. I am not capable of doing so. I cannot please them without wantonly violating not only my oath, but the most vital principles upon which our government was founded.

"As to those who, like Wade and the rest, see fit to depreciate my policy and cavil at my official acts, I shall not complain of them. I accord them the utmost freedom of speech and liberty of the press, but shall not change the policy I have adopted in the full belief that I am right.

"I feel on this subject as an old Illinois farmer once expressed himself while eating cheese. He was interrupted in the midst of his repast by the entrance of his son, who exclaimed, 'Hold on, dad! there's skippers in that cheese you're eating!'

"'Never mind, Tom,' said he, as he kept on munching his cheese, 'if they can stand it I can.'"

A MORTIFYING EXPERIENCE

A lady reader or elocutionist came to Springfield in 1857. A large crowd greeted her. Among other things she recited "Nothing to Wear," a piece in which is described the perplexities that beset "Miss Flora McFlimsey" in her efforts to appear fashionable.

In the midst of one stanza in which no effort is made to say anything particularly amusing, and during the reading of which the audience manifested the most respectful silence and attention, some one in the rear seats burst out with a loud, coarse laugh, a sudden and explosive guffaw.

It startled the speaker and audience, and kindled a storm of unsuppressed laughter and applause. Everybody looked back to ascertain the cause of the demonstration, and were greatly surprised to find that it was Mr. Lincoln.

He blushed and squirmed with the awkward diffidence of a schoolboy. What caused him to laugh, no one was able to explain. He was doubtless wrapped up in a brown study, and recalling some amusing episode indulged in laughter without realizing his surroundings. The experience mortified him greatly.

GRANT HELD ON ALL THE TIME

(Dispatch to General Grant, August 17th, 1864.)

"I have seen your dispatch expressing your unwillingness to break your hold where you are. Neither am I willing.

"Hold on with a bulldog grip."

EVERY LITTLE HELPED

As the time drew near at which Mr. Lincoln said he would issue the Emancipation Proclamation, some clergymen, who feared the President might change his mind, called on him to urge him to keep his promise.

"We were ushered into the Cabinet room," says Dr. Sunderland. "It was very dim, but one gas jet burning. As we entered, Mr. Lincoln was standing at the farther end of the long table, which filled the center of the room. As I stood by the door, I am so very short that I was obliged to look up to see the President. Mr. Robbins introduced me, and I began at once by saying: 'I have come, Mr. President, to anticipate the new year with my respects, and if I may, to say to you a word about the serious condition of this country.'

"'Go ahead, Doctor,' replied the President; 'every little helps.' But I was too much in earnest to laugh at his sally at my smallness."

KEPT UP THE ARGUMENT

Judge T. Lyle Dickey of Illinois related that when the excitement over the Kansas-Nebraska bill first broke out, he was with Lincoln and several friends attending court. One evening several persons, including himself and Lincoln, were discussing the slavery question. Judge Dickey contended that slavery was an institution which the Constitution recognized, and which could not be disturbed. Lincoln argued that ultimately slavery must become extinct. "After a while," said Judge Dickey, "we went upstairs to bed. There were two beds in our room, and I remember that Lincoln sat up in his night shirt on the edge of the bed arguing the point with me. At last we went to sleep. Early in the morning I woke up and there was Lincoln half sitting up in bed. 'Dickey', said he, 'I tell you this nation cannot exist half slave and half free.' 'Oh, Lincoln,' said I, 'go to sleep.'"

THOUGHT OF LEARNING A TRADE

Lincoln at one time thought seriously of learning the blacksmith's trade. He was without means, and felt the immediate necessity of undertaking some business that would give him bread. While entertaining this project an event occurred which, in his undetermined state of mind, seemed to open a way to success in another quarter.

Reuben Radford, keeper of a small store in the village of New Salem, had incurred the displeasure of the "Clary Grove Boys," who exercised their "regulating" prerogatives by irregularly breaking his windows. William G.

Greene, a friend of young Lincoln, riding by Radford's store soon afterward, was hailed by him and told that he intended to sell out. Mr. Greene went into the store, and offered him at random $400 for his stock, which offer was immediately accepted.

Lincoln "happened in" the next day, and being familiar with the value of the goods, Mr. Greene proposed to him to take an inventory of the stock, and see what sort of a bargain he had made. This he did, and it was found that the goods were worth $600.

Lincoln then made an offer of $125 for his bargain, with the proposition that he and a man named Berry, as his partner, take over Greene's notes given to Radford. Mr. Greene agreed to the arrangement, but Radford declined it, except on condition that Greene would be their security. Greene at last assented.

Lincoln was not afraid of the "Clary Grove Boys"; on the contrary, they had been his most ardent friends since the time he thrashed "Jack" Armstrong, champion bully of "The Grove"—but their custom was not heavy.

The business soon became a wreck; Greene had to not only assist in closing it up, but pay Radford's notes as well. Lincoln afterwards spoke of these notes which he finally made good to Greene, as "the National Debt."

THE SAME OLD RUM

One of President Lincoln's friends, visiting at the White House, was finding considerable fault with the constant agitation in Congress of the slavery question. He remarked that, after the adoption of the Emancipation policy, he had hoped for something new.

"There was a man down in Maine," said the President, in reply, "who kept a grocery store, and a lot of fellows used to loaf around for their toddy. He only gave 'em New England rum, and they drank pretty considerable of it. But after a while they began to get tired of that, and kept asking for something new—something new—all the time. Well, one night, when the whole crowd were around, the grocer brought out his glasses, and says he, 'I've got something New for you to drink, boys, now.'

"'Honor bright?' says they.

"'Honor bright,' says he, and with that he sets out a jug. 'Thar,' says he, 'that's something New; it's New England rum!' says he.

"Now," remarked the President, in conclusion, "I guess we're a good deal like that crowd, and Congress is a good deal like that store-keeper!"

COULDN'T LET GO THE HOG

When Governor Custer of Pennsylvania described the terrible butchery at the battle of Fredericksburg, Mr. Lincoln was almost broken-hearted.

The Governor regretted that his description had so sadly affected the President. He remarked: "I would give all I possess to know how to rescue you from this terrible war." Then Mr. Lincoln's wonderful recuperative powers asserted themselves and this marvelous man was himself.

Lincoln's whole aspect suddenly changed, and he relieved his mind by telling a story.

"This reminds me, Governor," he said, "of an old farmer out in Illinois that I used to know.

"He took it into his head to go into hog-raising. He sent out to Europe and imported the finest breed of hogs he could buy.

"The prize hog was put in a pen, and the farmer's two mischievous boys, James and John, were told to be sure not to let it out. But James, the worst of the two, let the brute out the next day. The hog went straight for the boys, and drove John up a tree; then the hog went for the seat of James' trousers, and the only way the boy could save himself was by holding on to the hog's tail.

"The hog would not give up his hunt, nor the boy his hold! After they had made a good many circles around the tree, the boy's courage began to give out, and he shouted to his brother, 'I say, John, come down quick, and help me let go this hog!'

"Now, Governor, that is exactly my case. I wish some one would come and help me to let the hog go."

HIS KNOWLEDGE OF HUMAN NATURE

Once, when Lincoln was pleading a case, the opposing lawyer had all the advantage of the law; the weather was warm, and his opponent, as was admissible in frontier courts, pulled off his coat and vest as he grew warm in the argument.

At that time, shirts with buttons behind were unusual. Lincoln took in the situation at once. Knowing the prejudices of the primitive people against pretension of all sorts, or any affectation of superior social rank, arising, he said: "Gentlemen of the jury, having justice on my side, I don't think you will be at all influenced by the gentleman's pretended knowledge of the law, when you see he does not even know which side of his shirt should be in front." There was a general laugh, and Lincoln's case was won.

TOOK NOTHING BUT MONEY

During the War Congress appropriated $10,000 to be expended by the President in defending United States Marshals in cases of arrests and seizures where the legality of their actions was tested in the courts. Previously the Marshals sought the assistance of the Attorney-General indefending them, but when they found that the President had a fund for that purpose they sought to control the money.

In speaking of these Marshals one day, Mr. Lincoln said:

"They are like a man in Illinois, whose cabin was burned down, and, according to the kindly custom of early days in the West, his neighbors all contributed something to start him again. In his case they had been so liberal that he soon found himself better off than before the fire, and he got proud. One day a neighbor brought him a bag of oats, but the fellow refused it with scorn.

"'No,' said he, 'I'm not taking oats now. I take nothing but money.'"

CREDITOR PAID DEBTOR'S DEBT

A certain rich man in Springfield, Illinois, sued a poor attorney for $2.50, and Lincoln was asked to prosecute the case. Lincoln urged the creditor to let the matter drop, adding, "You can make nothing out of him, and it will cost you a good deal more than the debt to bring suit." The creditor was still determined to have his way, and threatened to seek some other attorney. Lincoln then said, "Well, if you are determined that suit should be brought, I will bring it; but my charge will be $10."

The money was paid him, and peremptory orders were given that the suit be brought that day. After the client's departure, Lincoln went out of the office, returning in about an hour with an amused look on his face. Asked what pleased him, he replied, "I brought suit against — —, and then hunted him up, told him what I had done, handed him half of the $10, and we went over to the squire's office. He confessed judgment and paid the bill."

Lincoln added that he didn't see any other way to make things satisfactory for his client as well as the other.

CONSCRIPTING DEAD MEN

Mr. Lincoln being found fault with for making another "call," said that if the country required it, he would continue to do so until the matter stood as described by a Western provost marshal, who says:

"I listened a short time since to a butternut-clad individual, who succeeded in making good his escape, expatiate most eloquently on the rigidness with which the conscription was enforced south of the Tennessee River. His response to a question propounded by a citizen ran somewhat in this wise:

"'Do they conscript close over the river?'

"'Stranger, I should think they did! They take every man who hasn't been dead more than two days!'

"If this is correct, the Confederacy has at least a ghost of a chance left."

And of another, a Methodist minister in Kansas, living on a small salary, who was greatly troubled to get his quarterly instalment. He at last told the non-paying trustees that he must have his money, as he was suffering for the necessaries of life.

"Money!" replied the trustees; "you preach for money? We thought you preached for the good of souls!"

"Souls!" responded the reverend; "I can't eat souls; and if I could it would take a thousand such as yours to make a meal!"

"That soul is the point, sir," said the President.

MAJOR ANDERSON'S BAD MEMORY

Among the men whom Captain Lincoln met in the Black Hawk campaign were Lieutenant-Colonel Zachary Taylor, Lieutenant Jefferson Davis, President of the Confederacy, and Lieutenant Robert Anderson, all of the United States Army.

Judge Arnold, in his "Life of Abraham Lincoln," relates that Lincoln and Anderson did not meet again until some time in 1861. After Anderson had evacuated Fort Sumter, on visiting Washington, he called at the White House to pay his respects to the President. Lincoln expressed his thanks to Anderson for his conduct at Fort Sumter, and then said:

"Major, do you remember of ever meeting me before?"

"No, Mr. President, I have no recollection of ever having had that pleasure."

"My memory is better than yours," said Lincoln; "you mustered me into the service of the United States in 1832, at Dixon's Ferry, in the Black Hawk War."

SETTLED OUT OF COURT

When Abe Lincoln used to be drifting around the country, practicing law in Fulton and Menard counties, Illinois, an old fellow met him going to Lewiston, riding a horse which, while it was a serviceable enough animal, was not of the kind to be truthfully called a fine saddler. It was a weatherbeaten nag, patient and plodding, and it toiled along with Abe—and Abe's books, tucked away in saddle-bags, lay heavy on the horse's flank.

"Hello, Uncle Tommy," said Abe.

"Hello, Abe," responded Uncle Tommy. "I'm powerful glad to see ye, Abe, fer I'm gwyne to have sumthin' fer ye at Lewiston co't, I reckon."

"How's that, Uncle Tommy?" said Abe.

"Well, Jim Adams, his land runs 'long o' mine, he's pesterin' me a heap, an' I got to get the law on Jim, I reckon."

"Uncle Tommy, you haven't had any fights with Jim, have you?"
"No."

"He's a fair to middling neighbor, isn't he?" "Only tollable, Abe."

"He's been a neighbor of yours for a long time, hasn't he?"
"Nigh on to fifteen year."

"Part of the time you get along all right, don't you?" "I

reckon we do, Abe."

"Well, now, Uncle Tommy, you see this horse of mine? He isn't as good a horse as I could straddle, and I sometimes get out of patience with him, but I know his faults. He does fairly well as horses go, and it might take me a long time to get used to some other horse's faults. For all horses have faults. You and Uncle Jimmy must put up with each other, as I and my horse do with one another."

"I reckon, Abe," said Uncle Tommy, as he bit off about four ounces of Missouri plug, "I reckon you're about right."

And Abe Lincoln, with a smile on his gaunt face, rode on toward Lewiston.

NO VANDERBILT

In February, 1860, not long before his nomination for the Presidency, Lincoln made several speeches in Eastern cities. To an Illinois acquaintance, whom he met at the Astor House, in New York, he said:

"I have the cottage at Springfield, and about three thousand dollars in money. If they make me Vice-President with Seward, as some say they will, I hope I shall be able to increase it to twenty thousand, and that is as much as any man ought to want."

LINCOLN MISTAKEN FOR ONCE

President Lincoln was compelled to acknowledge that he made at least one mistake in "sizing up" men. One day a very dignified man called at the White House, and Lincoln's heart fell when his visitor approached. The latter was portly, his face was full of apparent anxiety, and Lincoln was willing to wager a year's salary that he represented some Society for the Easy and Speedy Repression of Rebellions.

The caller talked fluently, but at no time did he give advice or suggest a way to put down the Confederacy. He was full of humor, told a clever story or two, and was entirely self-possessed.

At length the President inquired, "You are a clergyman, are you not, sir?"

"Not by a jug full," returned the stranger heartily.

Grasping him by the hand Lincoln shook it until the visitor squirmed. "You must lunch with us. I am glad to see you. I was afraid you were a preacher."

"I went to the Chicago Convention," the caller said, "as a friend of Mr. Seward. I have watched you narrowly ever since your inauguration, and I called merely to pay my respects. What I want to say is this: I think you are doing everything for the good of the country that is in the power of man to do. You are on the right track. As one of your constituents I now say to you, do in future as you d— — please, and I will support you!"

This was spoken with tremendous effect.

"Why," said Mr. Lincoln, in great astonishment, "I took you to be a preacher. I thought you had come here to tell me how to take Richmond," and he again grasped the hand of his strange visitor.

Accurate and penetrating as Mr. Lincoln's judgment was concerning men, for once he had been wholly mistaken. The scene was comical in the extreme. The two men stood gazing at each other. A smile broke from the lips of the solemn wag and rippled over the wide expanse of his homely face like sunlight overspreading a continent, and Mr. Lincoln was convulsed with laughter.

He stayed to lunch.

"DONE WITH THE BIBLE"

Lincoln never told a better story than this:

A country meeting-house, that was used once a month, was quite a distance from any other house.

The preacher, an old-line Baptist, was dressed in coarse linen pantaloons, and shirt of the same material. The pants, manufactured after the old fashion, with baggy legs, and a flap in the front, were made to attach to his frame without the aid of suspenders.

A single button held his shirt in position, and that was at the collar. He rose up in the pulpit, and with a loud voice announced his text thus: "I am the Christ whom I shall represent today."

About this time a little blue lizard ran up his roomy pantaloons. The old preacher, not wishing to interrupt the steady flow of his sermon, slapped away on his leg, expecting to arrest the intruder, but his efforts were unavailing, and the little fellow kept on ascending higher and higher.

Continuing the sermon, the preacher loosened the central button which graced the waistband of his pantaloons, and with a kick off came that easy-fitting garment.

But, meanwhile, Mr. Lizard had passed the equatorial line of the waistband, and was calmly exploring that part of the preacher's anatomy which lay underneath the back of his shirt.

Things were now growing interesting, but the sermon was still grinding on. The next movement on the preacher's part was for the collar button, and with one sweep of his arm off came the tow linen shirt.

The congregation sat for an instant as if dazed; at length one old lady in the rear part of the room rose up, and, glancing at the excited object in the pulpit, shouted at the top of her voice: "If you represent Christ, then I'm done with the Bible."

SATISFACTION TO THE SOUL

In the far-away days when "Abe" went to school in Indiana, they had exercises, exhibitions and speaking-meetings in the schoolhouse or the church, and "Abe" was the "star." His father was a Democrat, and at that time "Abe" agreed with his parent. He would frequently make political and other speeches to the boys and explain tangled questions.

Booneville was the county seat of Warrick county, situated about fifteen miles from Gentryville. Thither "Abe" walked to be present at the sittings of the court, and listened attentively to the trials and the speeches of the lawyers.

One of the trials was that of a murderer. He was defended by Mr. John Breckenridge, and at the conclusion of his speech "Abe" was so enthusiastic that he ventured to compliment him. Breckenridge looked at the shabby boy, thanked him and passed on his way.

Many years afterwards, in 1862, Breckenridge called on the President, and he was told, "It was the best speech that I, up to that time, had ever heard. If I could, as I then thought, make as good a speech as that, my soul would be satisfied."

HIS TEETH CHATTERED

During the Lincoln-Douglas debates of 1858, the latter accused Lincoln of having, when in Congress, voted against the appropriation for supplies to be sent the United States soldiers in Mexico. In reply, Lincoln said: "This is a perversion of the facts. I was opposed to the policy of the administration in declaring war against Mexico; but when war was declared I never failed to vote for the support of any proposition looking to the comfort of our poor fellows who were maintaining the dignity of our flag in a war that I thought unnecessary and unjust."

He gradually became more and more excited; his voice thrilled and his whole frame shook. Sitting on the stand was O. B. Ficklin, who had served in Congress with Lincoln in 1847. Lincoln reached back, took Ficklin by the coat-collar, back of his neck, and in no gentle manner lifted him from his seat as if he had been a kitten, and roared: "Fellow-citizens, here is Ficklin, who was at that time in Congress with me, and he knows it is a lie."

He shook Ficklin until his teeth chattered. Fearing he would shake Ficklin's head off, Ward Lamon grasped Lincoln's hand and broke his grip.

After the speaking was over, Ficklin, who had warm personal friendship with him, said: "Lincoln, you nearly shook all the Democracy out of me today."

PROFANITY AS A SAFETY-VALVE

Lincoln never indulged in profanity, but confessed that when Lee was beaten at Malvern Hill, after seven days of fighting, and Richmond, but twelve miles away, was at McClellan's mercy, he felt very much like swearing when he learned that the Union general had retired to Harrison's Landing.

Lee was so confident his opponent would not go to Richmond that he took his army into Maryland—a move he would not have made had an energetic fighting man been in McClellan's place.

It is true McClellan followed and defeated Lee in the bloodiest battle of the War—Antietam—afterwards following him into Virginia; but Lincoln could not bring himself to forgive the general's inaction before Richmond.

A STAGE-COACH STORY

The following is told by Thomas H. Nelson, of Terre Haute, Indiana, who was appointed minister to Chili by Lincoln:

Judge Abram Hammond, afterwards Governor of Indiana, and myself, had arranged to go from Terre Haute to Indianapolis in a stage-coach.

As we stepped in we discovered that the entire back seat was occupied by a long, lank individual, whose head seemed to protrude from one end of the coach and his feet from the other. He was the sole occupant and was sleeping soundly. Hammond slapped him familiarly on the shoulder, and asked him if he had chartered the coach that day.

"Certainty not," and he at once took the front seat, politely giving us the place of honor and comfort. An odd-looking fellow he was, with a twenty- five cent hat, without vest or cravat. Regarding him as a good subject for merriment, we perpetrated several jokes.

He took them all with utmost innocence and good nature, and joined in the laugh, although at his own expense.

After an astounding display of wordy pyrotechnics, the dazed and bewildered stranger asked: "What will be the upshot of this comet business?"

Late in the evening we reached Indianapolis, and hurried to Browning's hotel, losing sight of the stranger altogether.

We retired to our room to brush our clothes. In a few minutes I descended to the portico, and there descried our long, gloomy fellow traveler in the center of an admiring group of lawyers, among whom were Judges McLean and Huntington, Albert S. White and Richard W. Thompson, who seemed to be amused and interested in a story he was telling. I inquired of Browning, the landlord, who he was. "Abraham Lincoln, of Illinois, a member of Congress," was his response.

I was thunderstruck at the announcement. I hastened upstairs and told Hammond the startling news, and together we emerged from the hotel by a back door, and went down an alley to another house, thus avoiding further contact with our distinguished fellow traveler.

Years afterward, when the President-elect was on his way to Washington, I was in the same hotel looking over the distinguished party, when a long arm reached to my shoulder and a shrill voice exclaimed, "Hello, Nelson! do you think, after all, the whole world is going to follow the darned thing off?" The words were my own in answer to his question in the stage-coach. The speaker was Abraham Lincoln.

SENTINEL OBEYED ORDERS

A slight variation of the traditional sentry story is related by C. C. Buel. It was a cold, blusterous winter night. Says Mr. Buel:

"Mr. Lincoln emerged from the front door, his lank figure bent over as he drew tightly about his shoulders the shawl which he employed for such protection; for he was on his way to the War Department, at the west corner of the grounds, where in times of battle he was wont to get the midnight dispatches from the field. As the blast struck him he thought of the numbness of the pacing sentry, and, turning to him, said: 'Young man, you've got a cold job tonight; step inside, and stand guard there.'

"'My orders keep me out here,' the soldier replied.

"'Yes,' said the President, in his argumentative tone; 'but your duty can be performed just as well inside as out here, and you'll oblige me by going in.'

"'I have been stationed outside,' the soldier answered, and resumed his beat.

"'Hold on there!' said Mr. Lincoln, as he turned back again; 'it occurs to me that I am Commander-in-Chief of the army, and I order you to go inside.'"

"WUZ GOIN' TER BE 'HITCHED'"

"Abe's" nephew—or one of them—related a story in connection with Lincoln's first love (Anne Rutledge), and his subsequent marriage to Miss Mary Todd. This nephew was a plain, every-day farmer, and thought everything of his uncle, whose greatness he quite thoroughly appreciated, although he did not pose to any extreme as the relative of a President of the United States.

Said he one day, in telling his story:

"Us child'en, w'en we heerd Uncle 'Abe' wuz a-goin' to be married, axed Gran'ma ef Uncle 'Abe' never hed a gal afore, an' she says, sez she, 'Well, "Abe" wuz never a han' nohow to run 'round visitin' much, or go with the gals, neither, but he did fall in love with a Anne Rutledge, who lived out near Springfield, an' after she died he'd come home an' ev'ry time he'd talk 'bout her, he cried dreadful. He never could talk of her nohow 'thout he'd jes' cry an' cry, like a young feller.'

"Onct he tol' Gran'ma they wuz goin; ter be hitched, they havin' promised each other, an' thet is all we ever heered 'bout it. But, so it wuz, that arter Uncle 'Abe' hed got over his mournin', he wuz married ter a woman w'ich hed lived down in Kentuck.

"Uncle 'Abe' hisself tol' us he wuz married the nex' time he come up ter our place, an' w'en we ast him why he didn't bring his wife up to see us, he said: 'She's very busy and can't come.'

"But we knowed better'n that. He wuz too proud to bring her up, 'cause nothin' would suit her, nohow. She wuzn't raised the way we wuz, an' wuz different from us, and we heerd, tu, she wuz as proud as cud be.

"No, an' he never brought none uv the child'en, neither.

"But then, Uncle 'Abe,' he wuzn't to blame. We never thought he wuz stuck up."

Lector House believes that a society develops through a two-fold approach of continuous learning and adaptation, which is derived from the study of classic literary works spread across the historic timeline of literature records. Therefore, we aim at reviving, repairing and redeveloping all those inaccessible or damaged but historically as well as culturally important literature across subjects so that the future generations may have an opportunity to study and learn from past works to embark upon a journey of creating a better future.

This book is a result of an effort made by Lector House towards making a contribution to the preservation and repair of original ancient works which might hold historical significance to the approach of continuous learning across subjects.

HAPPY READING & LEARNING!

LECTOR HOUSE LLP
E-MAIL: lectorpublishing@gmail.com

www.ingramcontent.com/pod-product-compliance
Lightning Source LLC
LaVergne TN
LVHW090010200726
843493LV00004B/837